長崎 旧浦上天主堂
Nagasaki Urakami Cathedral, 1945-1958: An Atomic Bomb Relic Lost
1945-58 失われた被爆遺産

高原至…写真／横手一彦…文／ブライアン・バークガフニ…英訳
Photography: Takahara Itaru, Text: Yokote Kazuhiko, Translation: Brian Burke-Gaffney

岩波書店

はじめに

横手 一彦

　この写真集は、「長崎原爆」の爆心地から500メートルの地点にあって被爆し、崩壊した旧浦上天主堂の、その後の姿を記録したものである。写真にみとめられる被爆教会——鐘塔と南側壁の残塁は、1958年3月に解体撤去され、すでに存在しない。現在、私たちが浦上の小高い丘に仰ぎ見る美しい天主堂は、同じ場所に再建され、さらに改装を経た新しい建物である。

　撮影者の高原至は、1923年に長崎に生まれたカメラマンである。1945年3月の東京大空襲の時、東京の都心でB29爆撃機の胴体を真上に見上げながら逃げ、生き延びた。戦禍を避けて長崎に帰り、8月9日にさらに「長崎原爆」を体験した。それからの65年間、長崎を仕事の場とし、長崎の写真を撮り続けた。

　日本列島の最西端に位置する長崎県。その中心都市長崎市は、近世の鎖国政策の時代に、天領長崎として、清国やオランダとの交易が許された日本で唯一の港街であった。多くの石造アーチ橋で知られる長崎は、中島川の下流域に発達した街である。浦上は、水系は異なるものの中島川と同様に、市の北東部に水源を発して長崎港にそそぐ浦上川の下流域に位置する。それぞれの歴史性や文化性は異なっているのであるが、20世紀のはじめに浦上が長崎市に編入されたために、今日ではそのことがわかりにくくなっている。

　ザビエル渡来後の16世紀末、キリスト教文化の花が咲いた。宣教師とともにさまざまな富が流入し、長崎は栄えた。やがて徳川幕府のもと、キリスト教は邪教として禁じられ、鎖国政策が敷かれるように

戦前の浦上天主堂（撮影者不明、浦上天主堂所蔵）

Urakami Cathedral before World War II. (Photographer unknown, Urakami Cathedral)

Foreword

Yokote Kazuhiko

The present collection of photographs is a record of Urakami Cathedral, situated only 500 meters from the hypocenter and devastated by the heat and blast of the Nagasaki atomic bomb explosion. The belfry, southern wall and other remnants were demolished in March 1958 and now can be seen only in photographs. The beautiful building that a visitor sees today is the new Urakami Cathedral erected on the same site and subjected to further refurbishments in later years.

The photographer, Takahara Itaru, was born in Nagasaki in 1923. During the Tokyo air raids in March 1945 he fled for cover looking up at the American B29 bombers streaking over the center of the city. After that ordeal, he returned to Nagasaki only to experience the atomic bombing of August 9 the same year. In the six and a half decades since then, Nagasaki has been his hub of activity and the subject of his ongoing work.

Nagasaki Prefecture is located at the western edge of the Japanese archipelago. The capital city of Nagasaki was under the direct jurisdiction of the Tokugawa Shogunate during the long period of national isolation (1641-1859) and the only port in Japan open for foreign trade. The Chinese and Dutch established commercial facilities here and contributed to the eclectic culture of the town. Nakashima River, the canal around which the town developed, was spanned at tight intervals by European-style stone arch bridges. The town was also nourished by Urakami River, which flowed from mountains to the northeast into Nagasaki Harbor, with a village of the same name nestling on a hillside in the lower reaches of the river. The history and culture of Nagasaki and Urakami differ, but these distinctions were blurred by the amalgamation of Urakami into the municipality of Nagasaki in the early 20th century.

Christian culture flourished in Japan after the visit of St. Francis Xavier in the middle of the 16th century, and Nagasaki prospered as a receptacle for the wealth accompanying the arrival of Catholic missionaries and traders. Before long, however, the Tokugawa Shogunate banned the foreign religion and adopted a policy of national isolation. In spite of this drastic change, the villagers in the Urakami district, while outwardly renouncing Christianity, continued to keep the light of faith burning in private. For two and a half centuries,

天主堂内部、南側の小祭壇(戦前。撮影者不明、浦上天主堂所蔵)

The altar on the southern side of Urakami Cathedral before the atomic bombing. (Photographer unknown, Urakami Cathedral)

1945年8月9日午前11時2分、松山町上空で原子爆弾炸裂。浦上天主堂は爆心地から500メートルの所であった
（財団法人 長崎平和推進協会 写真資料調査部会所蔵）

An atomic bomb exploded in the sky over the Matsuyama-machi district of Nagasaki at 11:02 a.m., August 9, 1945. Urakami Cathedral was located only 500 meters from the hypocenter.
(Nagasaki Foundation for the Promotion of Peace)

なった。この時代においても、長崎に隣接する公領浦上山里村などの一帯は、表向きは踏絵などの制度に従いながらも、密かな信仰を守り続ける。浦上は250年にわたり、潜伏キリシタンの里であった。長い禁教下、天領長崎の華の影に浦上では過酷な宗教弾圧があり、特に幕末から明治初期にかけての弾圧「浦上四番崩れ」においては、三千人余の民がこの地を追われた。多くの者が拷問に命を落とし、なかには耐えかねて教えを捨てる者もいた。

　旧浦上天主堂は、こうした過酷な歴史を経てようやく信教の自由が認められた近代、かつて踏絵が行われた庄屋の屋敷跡に建てられた「神の家」であった。その赤煉瓦の一つひとつは、この地の信仰を受け継いだ人びとが、父祖の苦難を思いながら、質素な生活のなかで資金と労力を出し合い、30年の長きにわたって積み上げたものである。1925年、浦上天主堂は完成した。天主堂は浦上の地を見守り、人びとは生活に息づいた信仰を高らかに歌い上げた。

　この喜びの時から、わずかに20年後のことである。1945年8月9日に米軍機「ボックス・カー」は、第1目標都市の福岡県小倉市上空が悪条件であったために投下を断念し、第2目標都市の長崎市上空へと飛来した。人類史上二個目の原爆は、さらに本来の目標地点であった長崎市街の中心部をはずれ、市北部の浦上に投下された。強烈な熱線と巨大な爆風をともなった火球は、一瞬にして、400年近い信仰を結実させた「神の家」も破壊し、一帯は紅蓮の炎が包む地獄となった。浦上信徒1万2千名のうち、8500名が被爆死したと言われる。他方、天領長崎の時代から続く古い街並みは、街が三方の丘陵地に囲まれる地形のなかにあったため、甚大な被害を直接的に受けることはなかった。浦上への原爆投下は、幾つもの偶然が折り重なった悲劇であった。人びとはこれを「浦上五番崩れ」と呼び、新たに背負った苦難を過去の歴史に重ね、敗戦後の厳しい現実を生きたのである。

　被爆した人びとと同様に、廃墟となった天主堂は、原爆による凄まじい破壊の爪痕を残した姿のまま、この浦上の地に立ち続けた。高原至の写真は、廃墟となった天主堂が、その後の13年間、浦上の人びとの生活のなかにしっかりと根付いていた姿を捉えている。被爆した石像、子どもたちの無垢な姿、和装の花嫁姿、瓦礫を運ぶ職人たち。荒涼とした原子野の浦上の丘、そして復興を遂げつつある浦上の丘

Urakami was home to the "underground Christians," who persevered in the dark shadow of religious persecution lurking behind the glory of the international port of Nagasaki. This persecution reached a peak in the late 1860's when more than 3,000 villagers were uprooted and exiled to other parts of Japan, a tragedy know today as *yonban kuzure*—the "fourth collapse." Many of these people died from the effects of torture; others avoided death by recanting.

The former Urakami Cathedral was a "House of God" built in the wake of these terrible hardships when freedom of religion was finally granted, and it stood on the site of the former headman's residence where villagers had been regularly forced to prove their renunciation by stepping on Christian images. The bricks were piled up one by one over a period of 30 years, each an expression of reverence for the sacrifice of ancestors molded from the simple resources and backbreaking work of the people. When the construction finally reached completion in 1925, the cathedral looked over the rooftops of Urakami and watched the people celebrate joyfully and confirm their unremitting faith.

Only 20 years had elapsed on August 9, 1945. An American bomber nicknamed "Bock's Car" abandoned its primary target—the industrial city of Kokura in Fukuoka Prefecture—because of bad weather and proceeded to the sky over the reserve target of Nagasaki. The airplane failed to pinpoint the planned target point in the center of the city and instead flew northward and dropped the second atomic bomb into the sky over the Urakami district. The explosion of this bomb generated ferocious heat rays and a tremendous blast that instantly destroyed the "House of God"—the fruition of four centuries of faith and sacrifice—and turned the Urakami area into a hellish sea of fire. It is estimated that 8,500 of the 12,000 Urakami parishioners perished in the atomic bombing.

On the other hand, the old neighborhoods in the central part of Nagasaki, shielded by mountains on three sides, escaped the full brunt of destruction. In this way, the explosion of the atomic bomb over Urakami was fraught with chance and error. Some people alluded to the event as a "fifth collapse" foisted upon the shoulders of the people of Urakami, who now faced the grim reality of life in the atomic wasteland.

The carcass of Urakami Cathedral blatantly revealed the scars of the atomic bomb, just like the people surviving in the ruined city. Takahara Itaru's photographs capture the carcass of the church as it settled into the lives of the people of Urakami over a period of 13 years. They show the damaged statues of saints, the innocent play of children, brides in traditional dress, and workers carrying away debris. They also highlight the contrast between the vivacious people of Urakami striving to restore their city and the ravaged remnants of the cathedral standing in the background.

南西から見た被爆後の天主堂。後に鐘塔と南側壁をのぞいて瓦礫は整理された。(1945年。林重男、長崎原爆資料館所蔵)

The carcass of Urakami Cathedral soon after the atomic bombing. The rubble was cleared away the following year, leaving only part of the belfry and southern wall standing. (1945. Photograph by Hayashi Shigeo. Nagasaki Atomic Bomb Museum)

爆風で崩落した鐘塔（1945年。撮影者不明、浦上天主堂提供）

The roof of the belfry toppled onto the ground as a result of the blast. (1945. Photographer unknown. Courtesy of Urakami Cathedral)

で、天主堂の崩れた外壁を背景に、朗らかに生きる人びとが鮮やかに写し出されている。その幾枚かは、被爆死した無名の人びとへの思いをかみしめ、また生活の再建に努める懸命な姿にうたれ、涙しながらレンズを向けたものであったという。高原至の写真は、現代史というものが、まぎれもなく、ここに写っているような一人ひとりの苦難によって編み上げた時間の束に他ならないことを教える。

そして写真はまた、1958年3月に、この被爆天主堂が解体撤去される過程をも記録している。この天主堂の存廃をめぐる議論は、この地のある年齢以上の人びとにとって、忘れることの出来ないものとして記憶されている。解体撤去の直前に開催された臨時市議会では、被爆の実相を伝える「全人類の20世紀の十字架」として残すべき、と最後まで主張し続けた議員もいた。しかし、残す、ということにはならなかった。

被爆から50年が経った1996年12月、広島原爆ドーム（旧県産業奨励館）が、ユネスコの世界遺産に登録された。一個目の原爆が投下された広島の廃墟に、「負の遺産」としての人類史的な意味付けがなされたのである。

もし、二個目の原爆が投下された被爆教会・旧浦上天主堂が、ここに写し出された姿のまま保存されていたのであれば、同じ意味付けがなされたであろう。天主堂は、被爆後の13年間、最も象徴的な被爆遺構であった。そして、半ば崩れ落ちた煉瓦壁や、鼻先や指先を爆風に吹き飛ばされ、熱線に傷ついた聖像たちは、あの瞬間の恐怖を、無言のうちに語り続けたに違いない。天主堂は、原爆の極限的な破壊をありのままに示した歴史遺産となったであろう。しかし今となっては、それは幻の世界遺産なのである。

筆者はこの写真集に、被爆した浦上天主堂の最後の姿——東洋一と呼ばれた戦前のそれよりもいっそう荘厳な姿をよみがえらせたいと願った。被爆後の時間のみならず、400年以上の長い時間軸において、浦上は、世界史的にも稀有な庶民史を織り成した地である。この写真集を通じて、旧浦上天主堂はなぜ失われたのか、あるいは「長崎原爆」という経験は何だったのかを問い直し、さらにそのような現代史からさかのぼって、この地にかつて生きた、あるいは生きようとした無数の名もなき人びとの姿を、透かし彫りのように浮かび上がらせることができれば、と考える。

The photographer remembers shedding tears when pushing the shutter button, moved by thoughts of the untold dead and by the sight of the tireless efforts of citizens to build a new life. Takahara Itaru's work confirms, beyond any shadow of doubt, that modern history is a brocade made from strands of hardship suffered by people just like those depicted in the photographs.

 The photographs also provide a vivid record of the demolition and removal of Urakami Cathedral in March 1958. Residents of a certain age can remember the arguments that raged over this issue. At an extraordinary meeting of the Nagasaki City Council held just before the demolition, some council members were still appealing for the preservation of the ruins as a "cross born by all humankind in the 20th century" and a testimony to the effects of nuclear weapons. However, the final decision did not fall in favor of preservation.

 In December 1996, the ruins of the Hiroshima Prefectural Industrial Promotion Hall—a structure commonly referred to as the "atomic bomb dome"—was registered on the UNESCO World Heritage List, an acknowledgment of the significance of the damage caused by the first atomic bomb as a negative legacy.

 If the ruins of Urakami Cathedral had been preserved, the significance for humanity would have undoubtedly been acknowledged in the same way. The carcass of the cathedral remained for 13 years as a symbolic and haunting reminder of the Nagasaki atomic bombing. The half-collapsed brick walls, like the statues with noses and fingers broken off by the blast, spoke silently but eloquently of the horror and atrocity of that fateful moment. If preserved, the ruins of the cathedral would have been an invaluable historic asset demonstrating the terrible destructive power unleashed by the atomic bomb. Today, however, they are phantoms lingering in the vault of memory.

 I envisioned the present collection as a way to resurrect the former Urakami Cathedral, which, in its ruined state, may have been even more resplendent with dignity and meaning than it had been as the grandest church in East Asia. Not just during the few years after the atomic bombing, but for more than four centuries, the people of Urakami experienced events unique in human history. I hope that Takahara Itaru's photographs provide an opportunity to ask why the ruins of Urakami Cathedral were lost and to inquire once again into the experience of the Nagasaki atomic bombing. I also hope that they shed light, like a carving in relief, on the faces of the countless, nameless people who lived here over the years.

All Japanese names in this book are rendered in the Japanese manner with the surname first.

瓦礫のなかの鐘。後に「長崎の鐘」と呼ばれる。(1945年。撮影者不明、浦上天主堂提供)

The bell in the ruins came to be called the "Bell of Nagasaki." (1945. Photographer unknown. Courtesy of Urakami Cathedral)

長崎市 1950年　Nagasaki, 1950

(「長崎」1:10000 都市計画図 長崎市近傍5号、1950年3月測図・6月印刷、長崎市。国立国会図書館蔵)

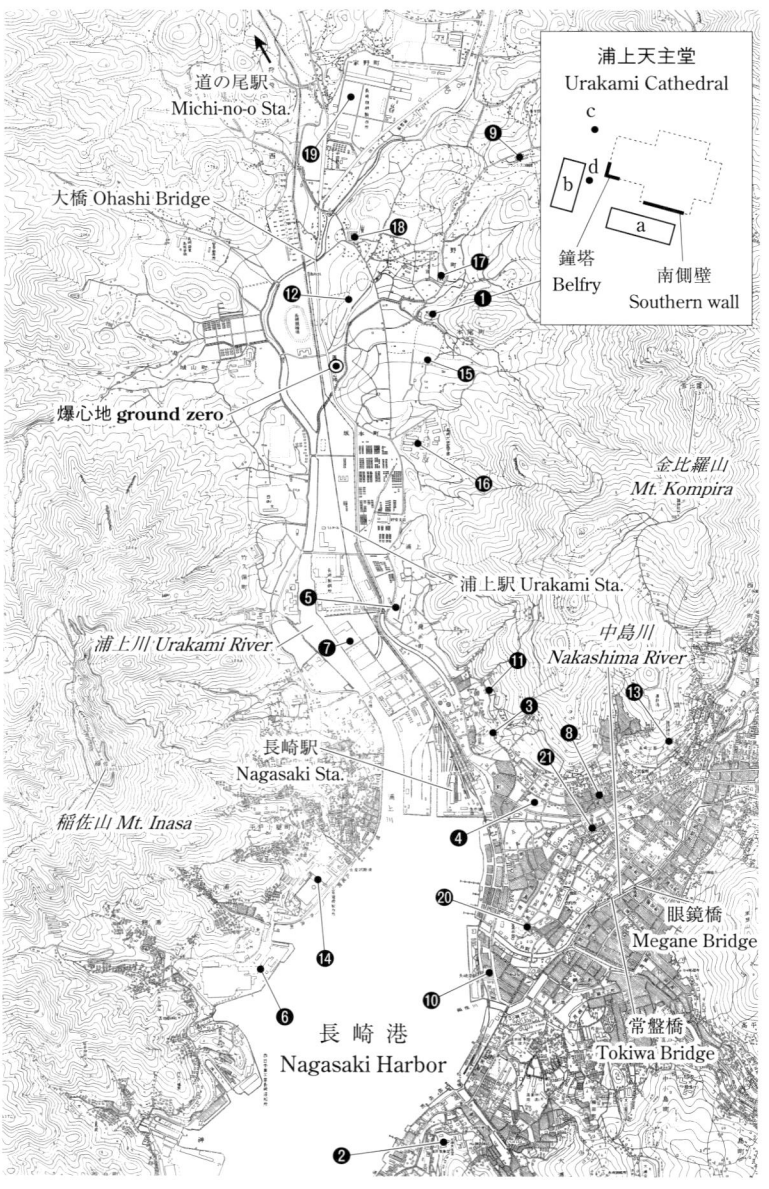

❶ 浦上天主堂 Urakami Cathedral
  a 仮聖堂 temporary church
  b 公民館 community center
  c 仮鐘楼 temporary bell tower
  d 信仰乃礎 "Pillar of Faith"
❷ 大浦天主堂 Oura Catholic Church
❸ 西坂公園 Nishizaka Park
❹ 西中町天主堂(現中町教会) Nishi-nakamachi Cathedral
❺ 聖徳寺 Shotokuji Temple
❻ 三菱造船所 Mitsubishi Shipyard
❼ *三菱兵器茂里町工場　Mitsubishi Arms Factory Mori-machi Plant
❽ 西勝寺 Saishoji Temple
❾ 浦上第一病院(現聖フランシスコ病院) Urakami Daiichi Hospital
❿ 長崎税関ビル Nagasaki Customs
⓫ *西坂国民学校(現西坂小学校) Nishizaka Primary School
⓬ *浦上刑務支所(現平和祈念像／平和公園) Urakami Branch Prison (present-day "Peace Statue" in Peace Park)
⓭ 諏訪神社 Suwa Shinto Shrine
⓮ 三菱電機製作所 Mitsubishi Electric Works
⓯ 長崎医科大学(現長崎大学医学部) Nagasaki Medical College
⓰ 長崎医大付属病院 Nagasaki Medical College Hospital
⓱ *常清高女 Josei Women's Vocational High School
⓲ *山里国民学校(現山里小学校) Yamazato Primary School
⓳ *三菱兵器大橋工場(現長崎大学文教キャンパス) Mitsubishi Arms Factory Ohashi Plant (present-day Nagasaki University campus)
⓴ 県庁 Prefectural Office
㉑ 市役所 City Hall

＊は戦前のもの。　＊prewar facility.

I
1949

I
1949

　長崎は、かつて日本の「小ローマ」といわれ、400年間絶えることなくキリスト教の信仰を受け継いだ地であった。
　被占領下にあっていまだ敗戦の傷跡も残る1949年。この年、聖フランシスコ・ザビエルの渡来400年を記念する国際的な式典が、被爆都市長崎で行われた。
　故国スペインに一度帰った以外はローマを離れたことのなかったザビエルの「聖腕」(右手)が、ガラスケースに収められて空輸された。世界3億人のカトリック信徒が関心を寄せ、日本に駐留していた連合軍総司令官マッカーサーが祝意の声明を発表した。
　5月29日午前9時、教皇特使一行と世界20ヵ国の代表、そして浦上信徒4千人と全国から参列した2万人の信徒が見守るなか、廃墟となった浦上天主堂の前で、野外ミサが行われた。その後、午後2時に大浦天主堂から西坂公園(26聖人殉教の地)に向け、小雨のなか市中を行列。浦上聖楽隊、聖歌隊、山口司教に奉持される「聖腕」を乗せた車、後続車に教皇名代シドニー大司教ギルロイ枢機卿、その後ろに信徒3万人余りの行列が続いた。その後特別列車が用意され、式典は鹿児島、大分、山口、広島、大阪などの由縁の地を巡り、6月12日に最終地東京の明治神宮外苑でミサが行われた。敗戦後初めての国際的な行事であった。

　　Known among early travelers as "Little Rome," Nagasaki served as a center of the Christian faith in Japan for four centuries.
　　In 1949, with the Occupation Period yet to end and the scars of war still painfully visible, an international celebration of the 400th anniversary of the arrival of St. Francis Xavier in Japan was held in Nagasaki.
　　The holy relic of Xavier's right forearm, which except for one visit to the saint's homeland of Spain had never been away from Rome, was flown to Nagasaki in a glass reliquary amid the good wishes of 300 million Catholic faithful worldwide. General Douglas MacArthur, commander of the Occupation Forces in Japan, also sent a message of felicitations on the occasion.
　　At 9:00 a.m. on May 29, 1949, some 20,000 people including a papal legate, representatives of 20 countries around the world, and more than 4,000 Urakami Catholics gathered for an outdoor Mass in front of the ruins of Urakami Cathedral. Around 2:00 p.m. the congregation proceeded in the rain from Oura Catholic Church to Nishizaka Park, site of the martyrdom of the Twenty-Six Saints of Japan in 1597. The procession was led by the Urakami Cathedral Brass Band and Chorus and cars with Bishop Yamaguchi Aijiro carrying the holy relic and Cardinal Norman Gilroy (papal legate and former archbishop of Sydney) and followed by more than 30,000 Catholic faithful. Over the following days, a special train was reserved to carry the representatives to Kagoshima, Oita, Yamaguchi, Hiroshima, Osaka and other related places in Japan, and a final pontifical high Mass was celebrated on June 12 at Meiji Shrine Outer Park Stadium in Tokyo. This was the first international event held in Japan in the wake of World War II.

かつての天主堂内部でおこなわれた野外ミサ。左端は、南側壁に設置された野外祭壇。背後の木造建築は仮聖堂(1946年建設)。中央、鐘塔の左背後には、公民館(1948年建設)。

The outdoor Mass was conducted in what was formerly the interior of the cathedral. An altar was established on the southern wall to the left. The temporary church (built in 1946) is visible in the background. Standing to the left behind the belfry is the community center built in 1948.

野外祭壇。右端に仮聖堂。

The outdoor altar. The temporary church is visible on the right.

野外祭壇。中央にザビエル像をあしらった十字架。

The outdoor altar, with a large cross and statue of St. Francis Xavier.

ザビエルの「聖腕」。特使の長崎滞在中、原爆の直接被害を受けなかった大浦天主堂に安置された。

The relic of St. Francis Xavier. During the stay of the papal legate in Nagasaki, the reliquary was placed in Oura Catholic Church, which had escaped destruction in the atomic bombing.

大浦天主堂前。ここから行列が出発した。

The procession departs from the front of Oura Catholic Church.

長崎市繁華街の行列。現在の観光通り。右上に岡政(現大丸デパート)が見える。車上に立って「聖腕」を持つのは山口愛次郎長崎司教。

The procession passes through downtown Nagasaki. The building in the right upper corner is Okamasa Department Store (present-day Daimaru). Standing in the open car and carrying the reliquary is Bishop Yamaguchi Aijiro.

西坂公園。遠くに西中町天主堂(現中町教会)が見える。

Nishizaka Park. The steeple of Nishi-nakamachi Church (present-day Nakamachi Church) is visible in the distance.

II
1953-54

II
1953-54

　1954年、日本は戦後復興の日々に別れを告げつつあった。経済企画庁が「もはや戦後ではない」と謳う2年前のことである。
　この年の3月、米国がビキニ環礁でおこなった水爆実験で、遠洋操業中のマグロ漁船第五福竜丸が被災し、日本は第三の被爆を経験する。これを契機として5月、杉並で原水爆禁止の署名運動がおこり、翌年の第1回原水爆禁止世界大会開催につながる。11月、水爆実験により目覚めた怪獣が東京を襲う映画『ゴジラ』が公開。敗戦後の新憲法は戦争放棄を宣言し、あらゆる軍の保持を禁止していたが、この年、陸海空自衛隊が発足した。
　浦上小教区の機関誌は、被爆後に1800名余りであった浦上信徒が、この頃には6500名余りとなったとしている(『あれの』第17号、1953年10月)。戦災復興事業による幾つもの土木工事がおこなわれ、焼け野原の浦上は、人びとがいきづく街へと大きく変わった。

　　By 1954 Japan was emerging from the days of postwar recovery, and within two years the Japanese government's economic planning agency would declare that "the postwar period is over."
　　In March, the crew of the tuna fishing steamer *No.5 Fukuryu-maru* was exposed to radioactive fallout from a hydrogen bomb test conducted by the United States in the Bikini Atoll. Japan's third experience of the wrath of nuclear weapons, this event sparked a campaign for a ban on atomic and hydrogen bombs in Suginami in May and paved the way to the First World Conference Against Atomic and Hydrogen Bombs held the following year. Unveiled in November, the movie *Gojira* (Godzilla) depicted a giant monster, awoken from slumber by a hydrogen bomb test, attacking the city of Tokyo. Although the new postwar constitution declared Japan's renunciation of war and ban on all military forces, the government of this country launched the "Japan Self-Defense Forces" in 1954.
　　According to a booklet published by the Urakami diocese, the Catholic residents of Urakami, reduced in number to little more than 1,800 after the atomic bombing, had increased to more than 6,500 by this time (*Areno*, Vol. 17, October 1953). Several civil engineering projects were underway as part of the postwar restoration effort, and the atomic wasteland was returning rapidly to a bustling city neighborhood.

右写真：南側壁。アーチ形玄関の左側に「悲しみの聖母像」、右側に「使徒聖ヨハネ像」。アーチは強烈な熱と爆風によって台座がずれ、柱には亀裂が生じている。左上は「聖チェチリア像」。

Statues of Mary in Mourning and St. John the Apostle stand at the arched portal of the southern wall. The tremendous heat and blast shifted the foundation stones and broke the column. The statue of St. Cecilia is visible on the upper left.

「悲しみの聖母像」。放射熱で黒く焼け焦げた。

The statue of Mary in Mourning. The surface was blackened by the heat rays.

「使徒聖ヨハネ像」。

Statue of St. John the Apostle.

「聖アグネス像」。1983年9月、求めにより、国連の原爆禍展示コーナーに収蔵された。

In September 1983, the statue of St. Agnes, shown here in the ruins, was moved to the atomic bomb exhibition space in the U.N. Headquarters in New York.

鐘塔、西側。

The western side of the belfry.

鐘塔の南側角から仮鐘楼を望む。花十字彫刻の石の上に置かれた天使半身像。

The view from the southern corner of the belfry, with the temporary bell tower to the left. The head of an angel has been placed on a stone with a floral design.

仮鐘楼に据え付けられた「長崎の鐘」。最初は丸太組みであったが、1946年に鉄骨造りに作り替えられた。この鐘は、現在の天主堂の向かって右の鐘塔にあり、浦上の丘に同じ音色を鳴り響かせる。1953年撮影。

The "Bell of Nagasaki" was suspended from a temporary tower made first of logs but replaced in 1946 with an iron frame structure. Today, this bell hangs in the right belfry of the new cathedral, and its rich familiar sound echoes over the rooftops of Urakami. Taken in 1953.

「長崎は生きていた。ああ、また、花が咲いた。平和がよみがえった、という気がした」(撮影者)。1953年撮影。

"Nagasaki was still alive. Flowers bloomed again! I felt as though peace had finally returned." (Photographer's words) Taken in 1953.

「声をあげて遊んでいる子どもたちを見ていると涙がこぼれ、光が見えたような気がした」(撮影者)。1953年撮影。

"My eyes filled with tears watching the children playing so happily. It was like a light in the darkness." (Photographer's words) Taken in 1953.

南側壁の残墟と聖像群。先生に引率され、輪になって元気に遊ぶ子供たち。

Remains of the southern wall and statues of the saints. Watched over by their teachers, children play happily in a circle.

いくたびも災禍に見舞われ、そのたびに復活を遂げたこの地。光を照らせば傍らに影が宿る。ここそこに、あの日消えた声がうずくまっている。

Urakami was a place of setback after setback, recovery after recovery. Beside each bright spot is a dark shadow. The sounds and voices of that fateful day are lost in silence.

III
1958

III
1958

1958 年、ついに解体の時が来た。

1958. The day of demolition was at hand.

扉写真：背景に 1955 年完成の平和祈念像が見える。新旧のモニュメントが同時に収まる貴重な写真。被爆の記憶を刻むのは、手前の廃墟。

This rare photograph captures both the old and the new: the memory of the atomic bombing engraved in the ruins of Urakami Cathedral, with the Peace Statue completed in 1955 pointing skyward in the background.

天主堂入口のスロープ。「旧聖堂廃墟の撤壊作業中 危険につき入場厳禁す 浦上教会」。1958年3月、解体撤去の作業が始まった。

The sign on the slope to the cathedral reads: "To prevent accidents, admission is strictly prohibited during the demolition of the ruined building." The removal of the ruins of Urakami Cathedral commenced in March 1958.

南側壁。左端に仮聖堂、奥は公民館。これらのものすべてが、被爆後に生き残った信徒の祈りを13年間受け止め、生きようとする心を支えた。

The southern wall with the temporary church to the left. The building in the background is the community center. For 13 years after the atomic bombing, these structures housed the prayers of the surviving faithful and inspired their efforts to recover.

天主堂の外壁を飾った14体の聖者石像の一つ。原石は天草石。

This is one of 14 statues of saints that decorated the cathedral exterior. The stone was quarried on Amakusa Island.

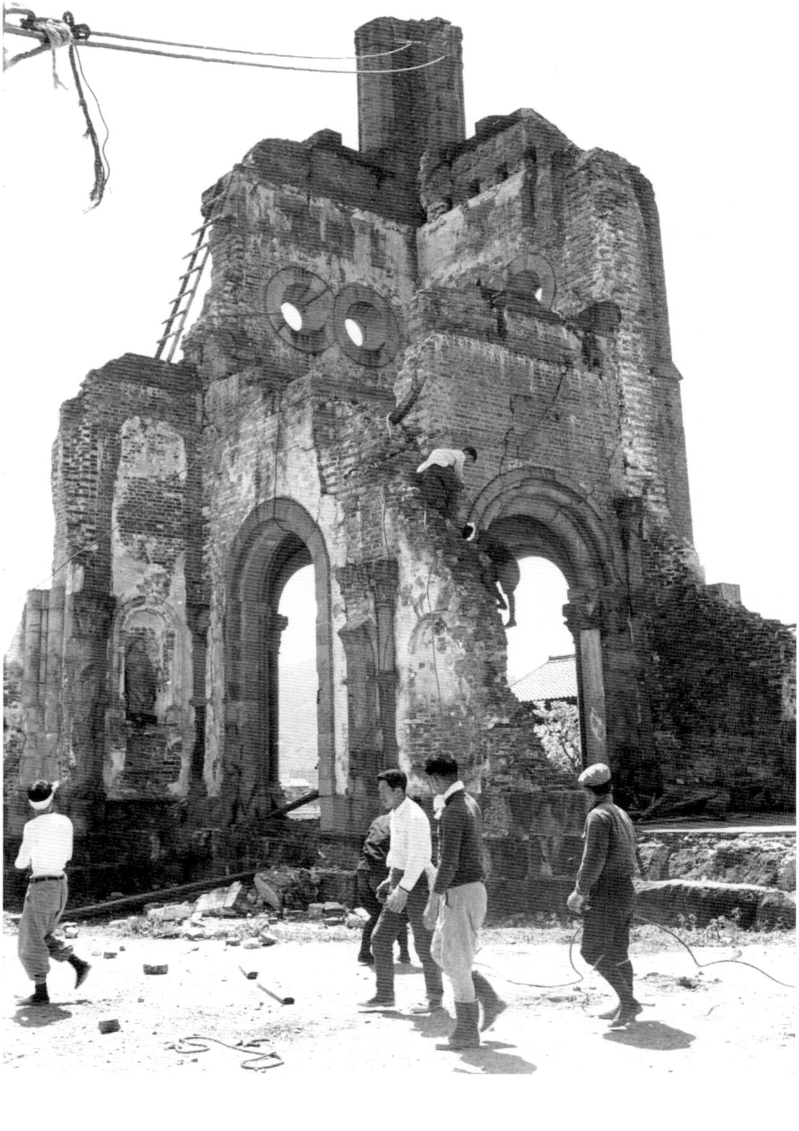

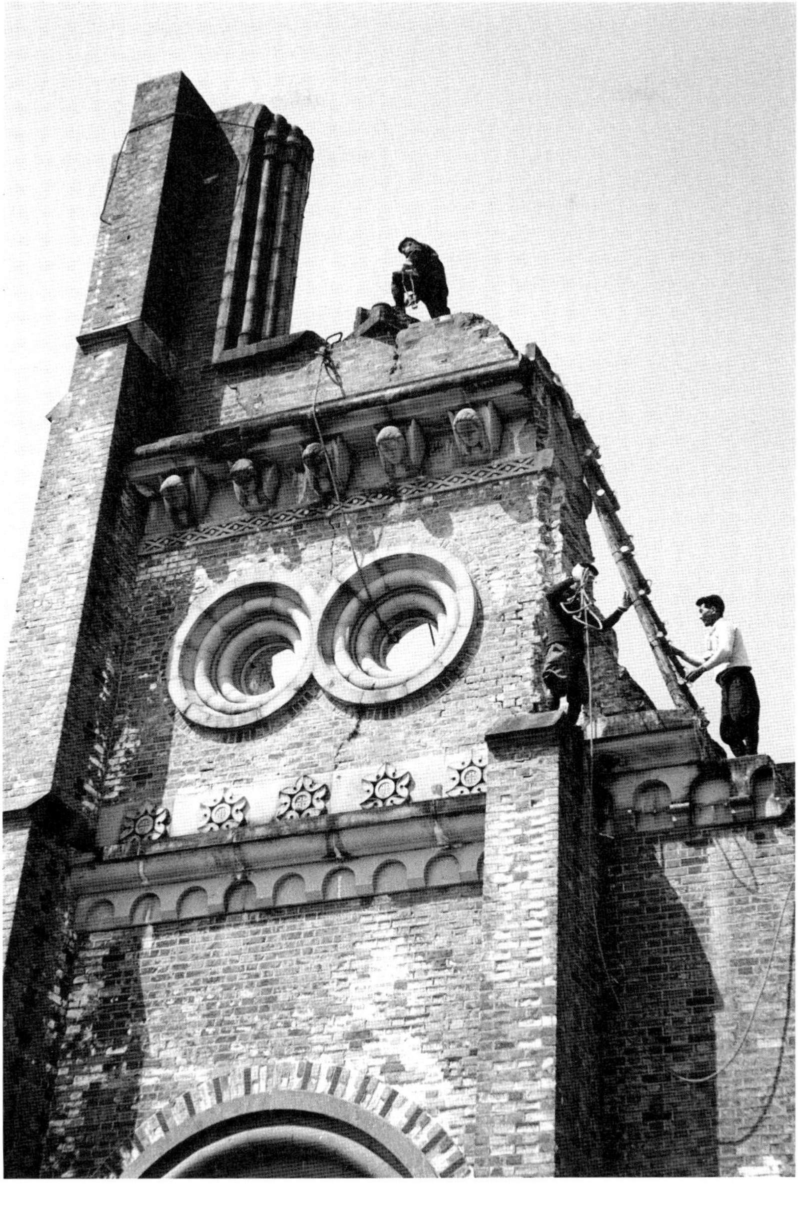

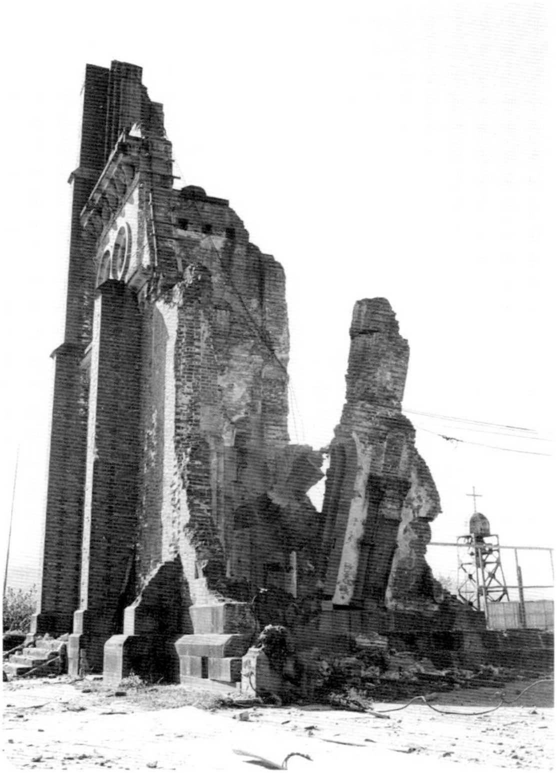

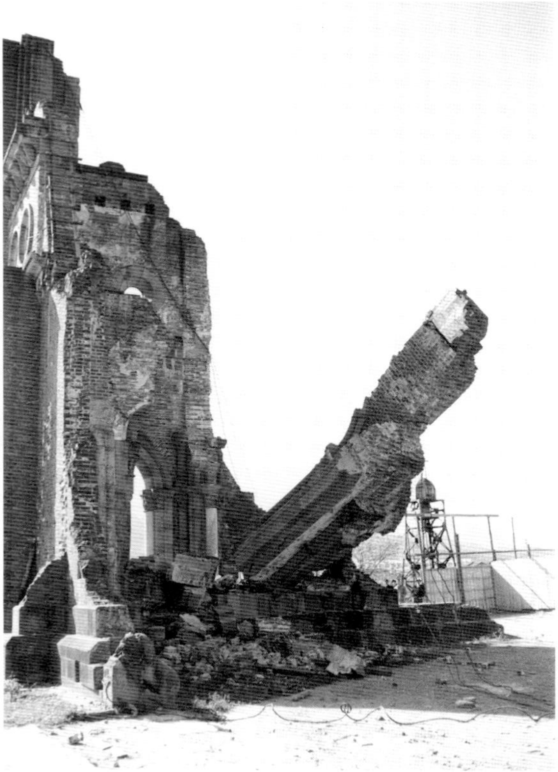

万力で倒される鐘塔の内部。奥に見えるのは、仮鐘楼。

Part of the old belfry is pulled to the ground with a vise. The temporary bell tower stands stoically in the background.

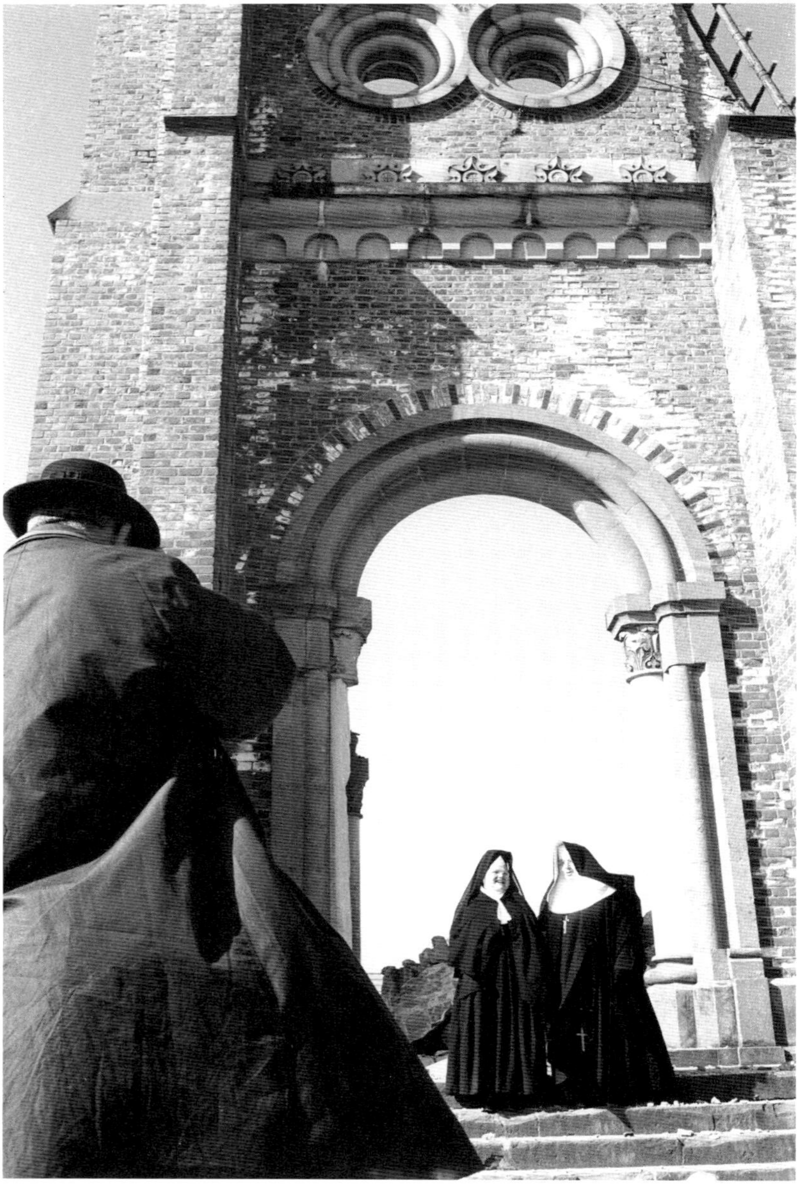

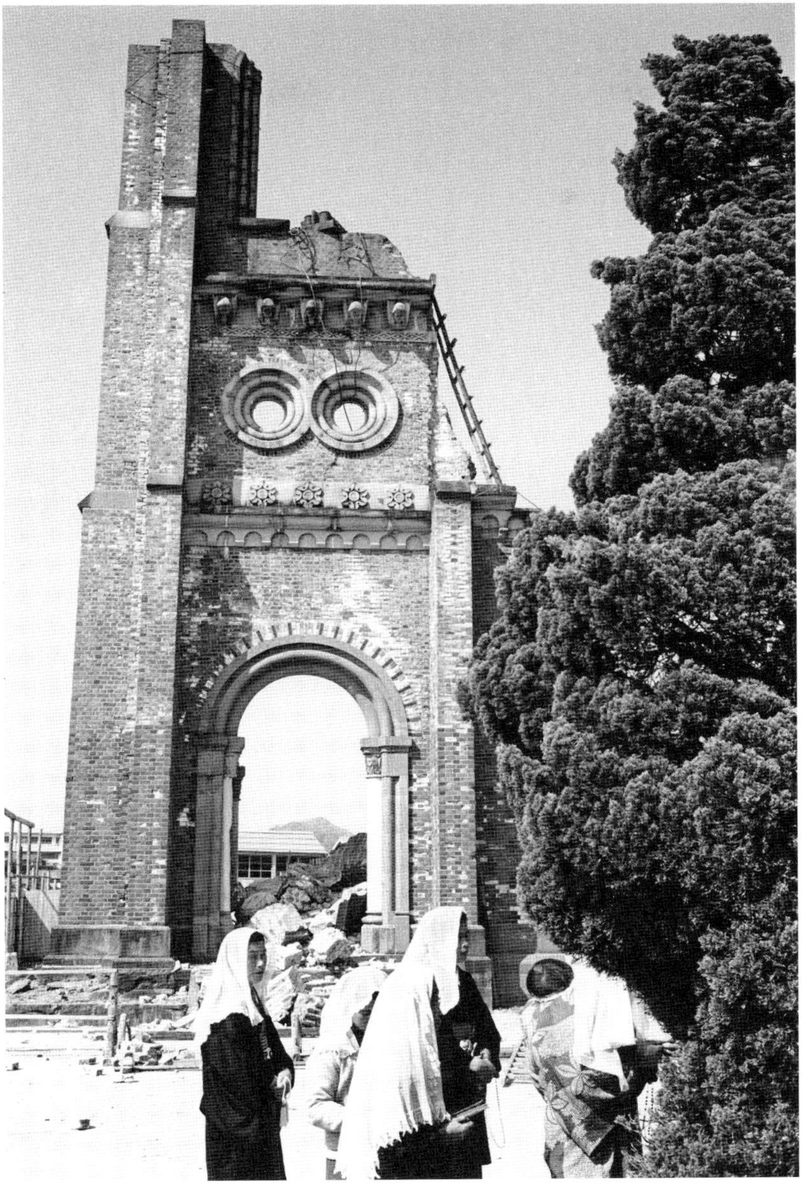

葬式の様子。

Scene from a funeral.

鐘塔の西側アーチ内部から。手前の天使半身像は、天主堂外壁の軒下を飾った84体の一つ。背後に「信仰乃礎」と、公民館。

This photograph was taken from inside the west arch of the belfry. The fallen statue is one of the 84 busts of angels installed under the eaves of the cathedral. The "Pillar of Faith" and community center are visible in the background.

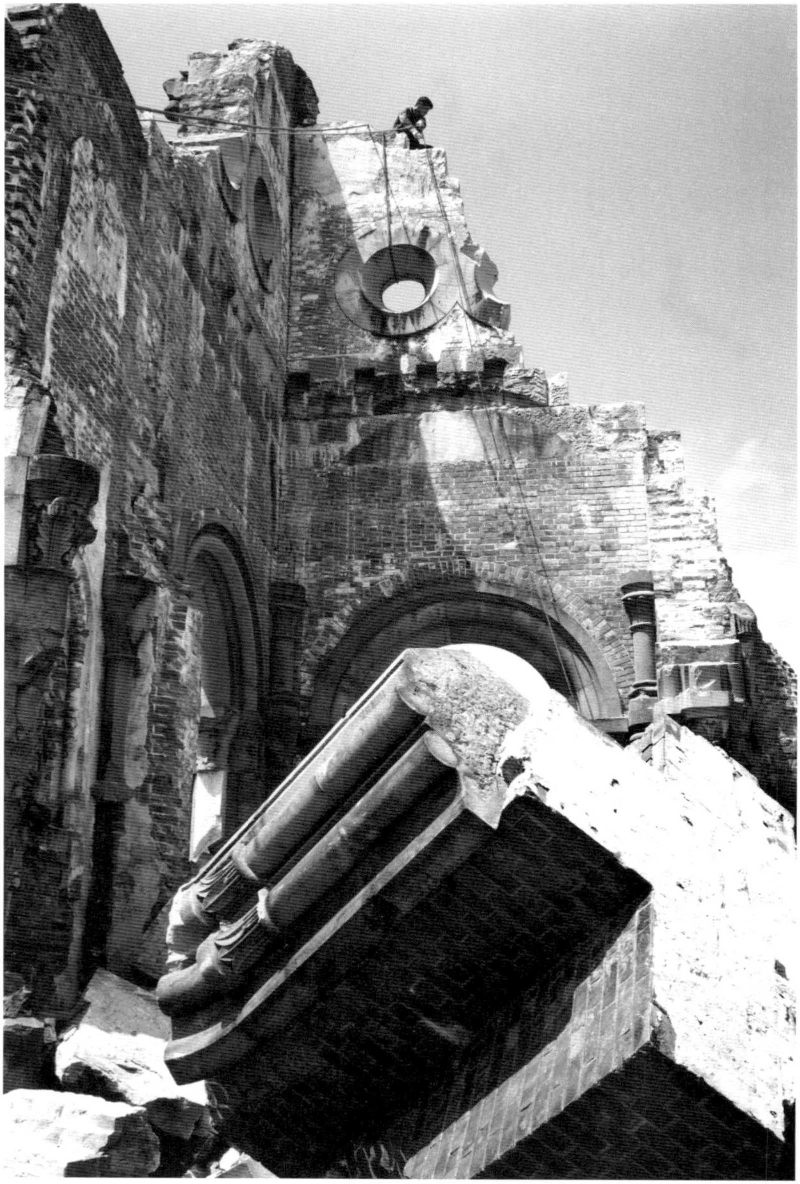

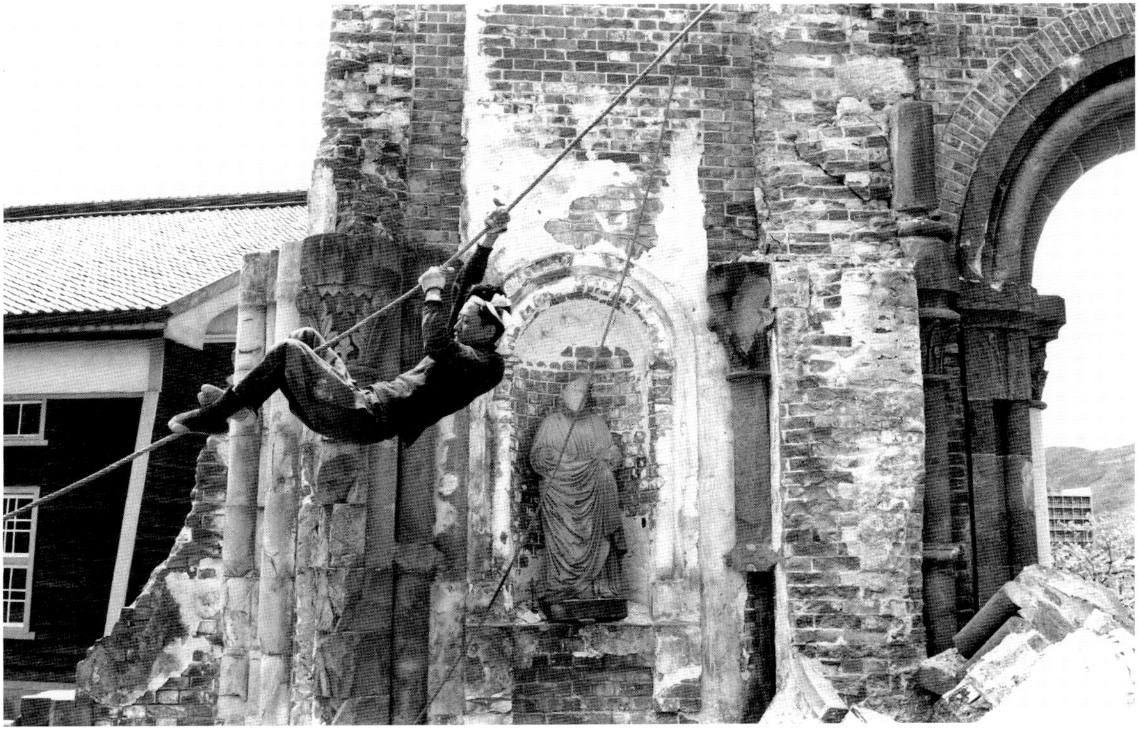

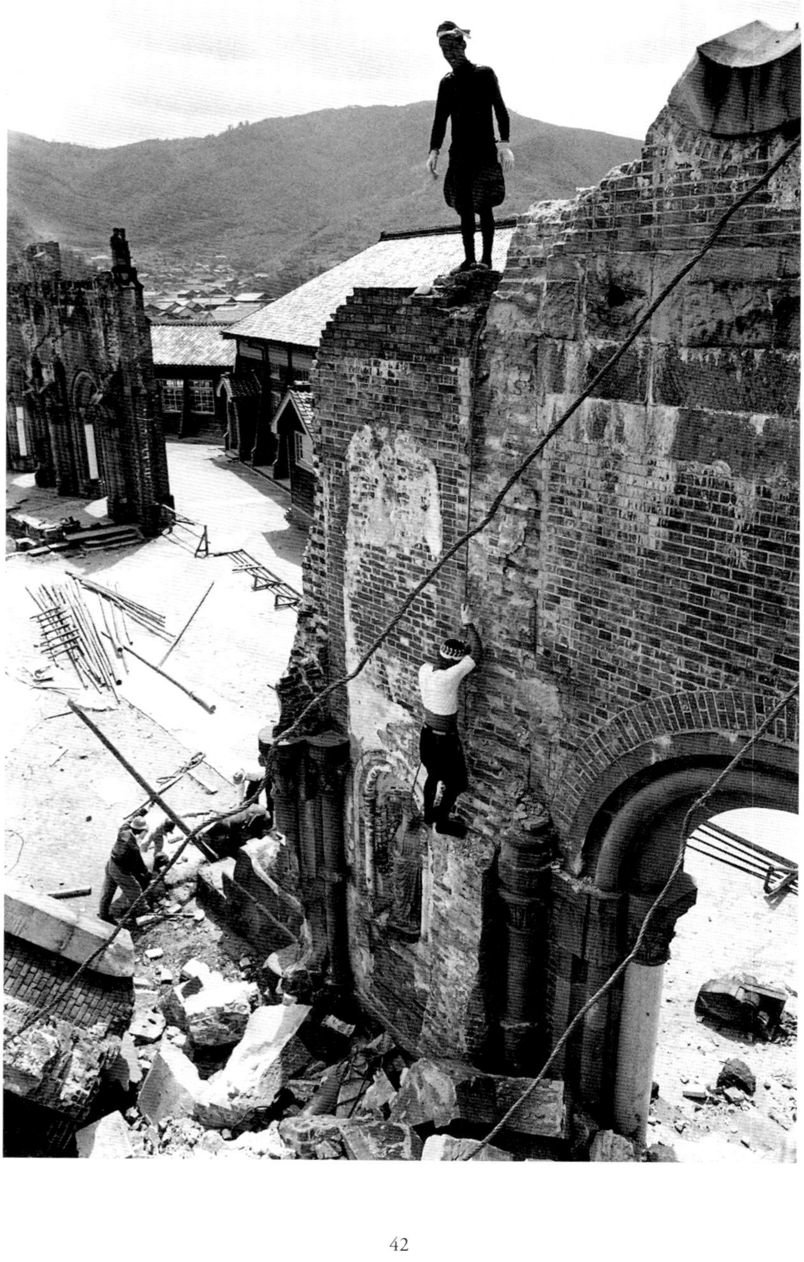

万力を使った解体作業。これを拒むかのように、堅牢な遺構は容易に壊れなかったといわれる。

A vise was used to complete the demolition work. It is said that the sturdy ruins gave way only reluctantly.

浜口健市神父。

Fr. Hamaguchi Kenichi.

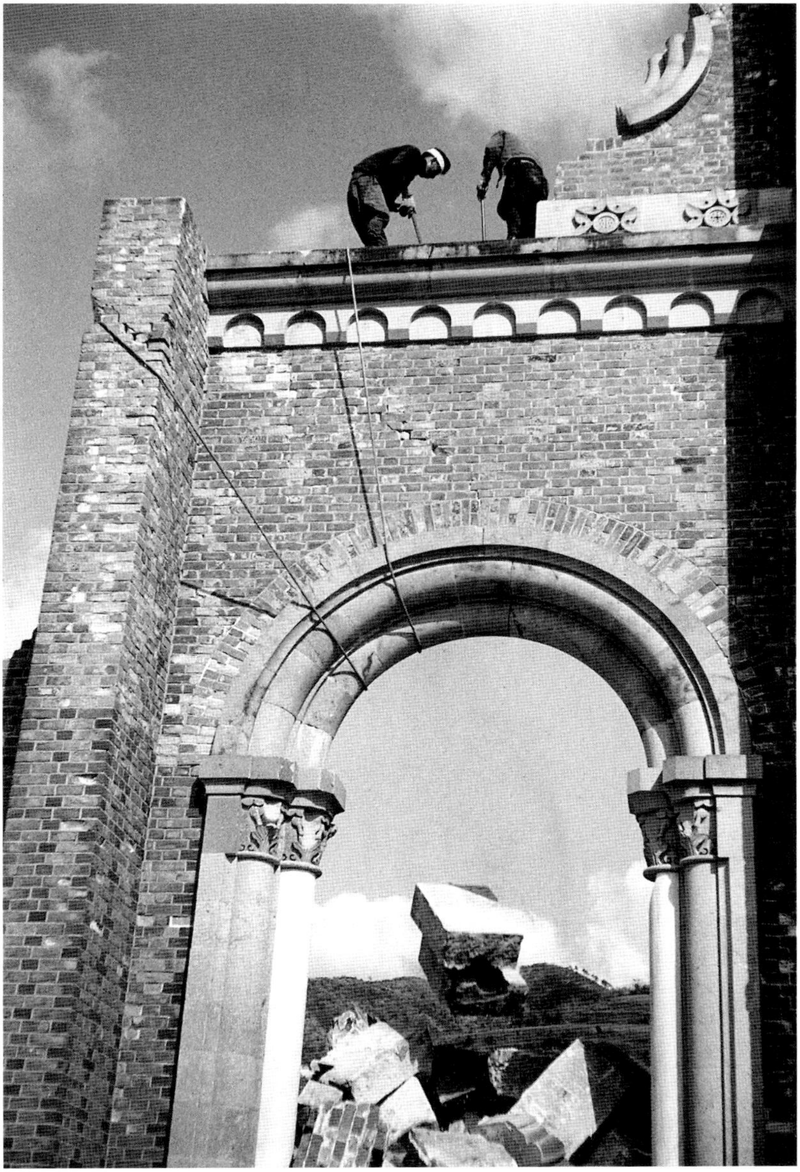

解体作業の多くは、ハンマーによる手作業であった。

Most of the demolition work was performed by hand using hammers.

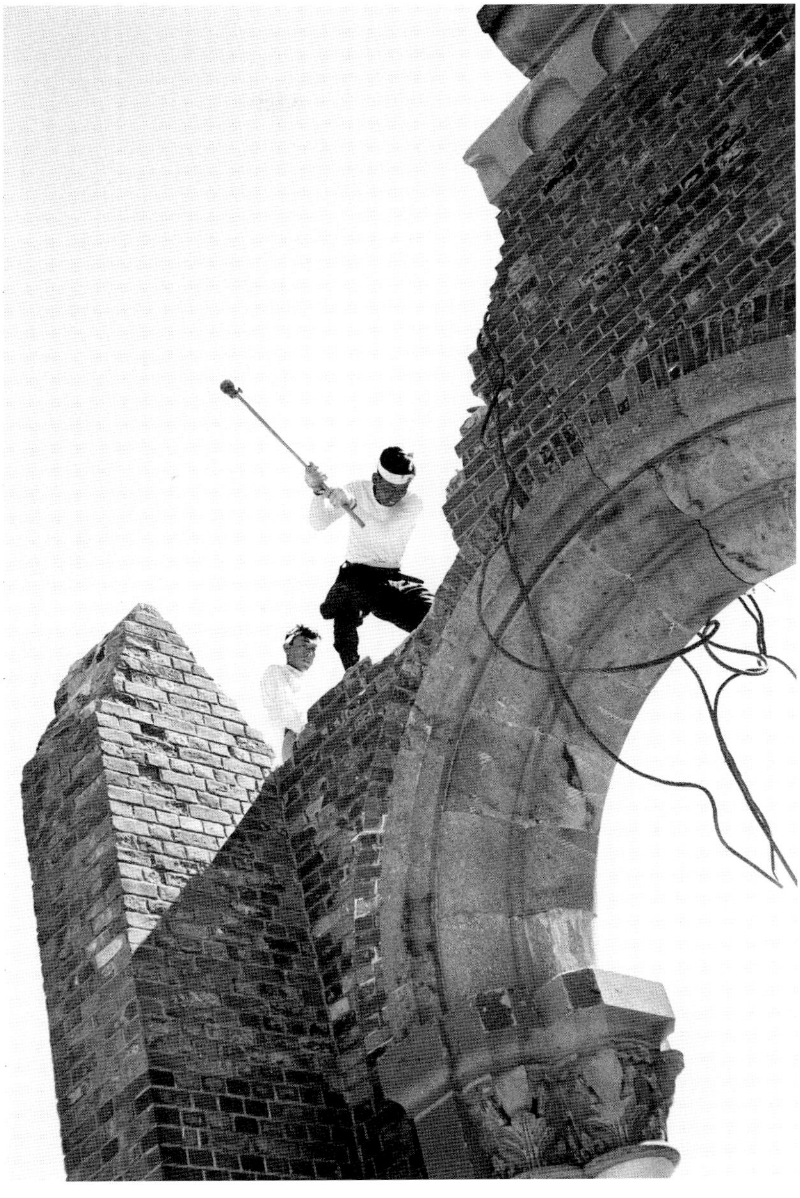

鐘塔をスケッチする男子生徒。作業のない休日の光景か。

A student sits in the shadow of the southern wall and sketches the belfry, apparently on a day when no work was underway.

花嫁と仲人。「廃墟からマリア様が出てきたと思い、夢中でシャッターを切った。また生きる力をもらった」(撮影者)。半世紀後の2009年、写真展をきっかけに、撮影者は花嫁に再び対面した。

A bride and her escort. "It was like a vision of Mary emerging from the ruins. I pushed the shutter button hurriedly, feeling as though I had been given another incentive to live." (Photographer's words) In 2009, the photographer met the bride during an exhibition of these photographs.

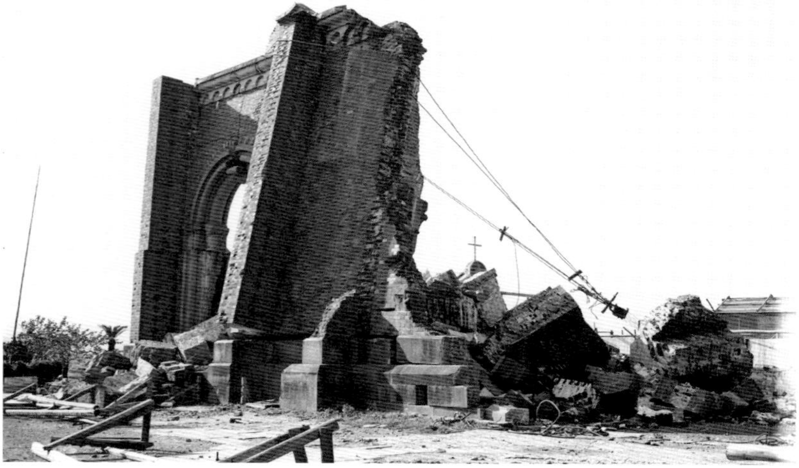

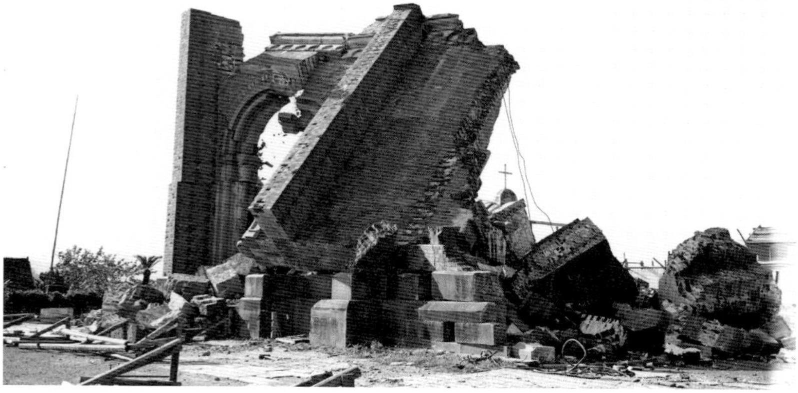

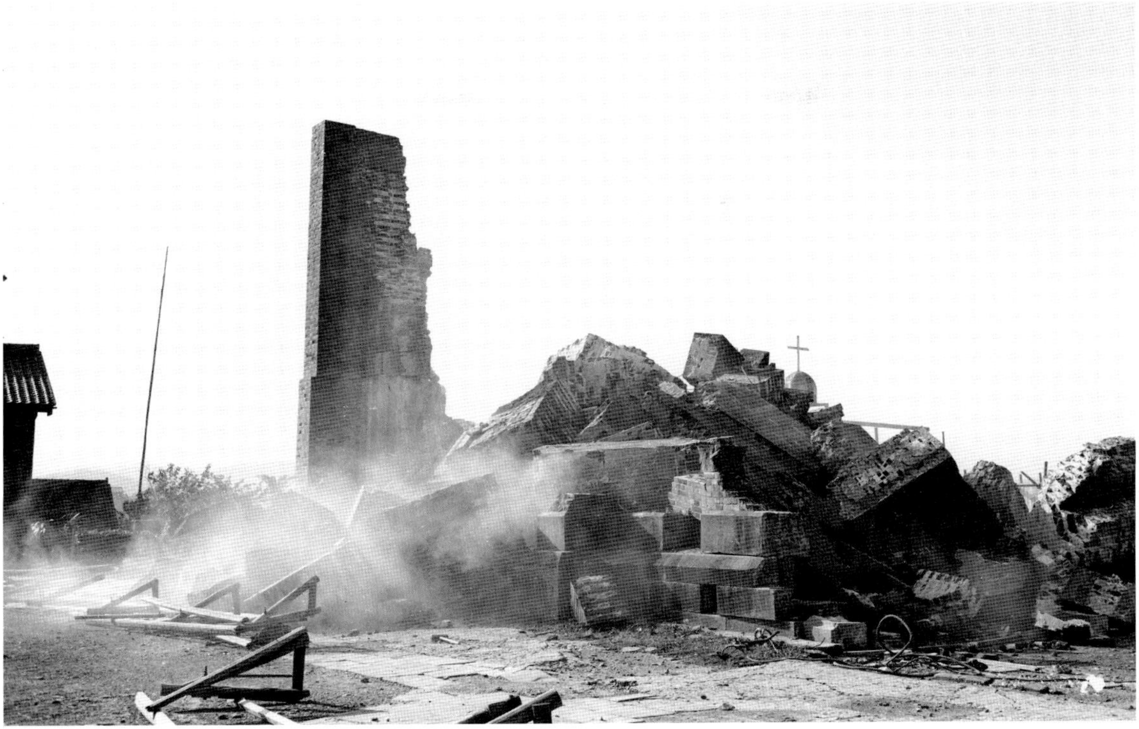

解体後の鐘塔瓦礫。積み上げられた瓦礫の向こうに見える十字架記念碑は「信仰乃礎」。1920年、浦上信徒総流配(浦上四番崩れ)50周年を記念して建立された。

The demolition work reduced the belfry to rubble. The monument with a cross visible behind the piled rubble is the "Pillar of Faith" erected in 1920 to commemorate the 50th anniversary of the eviction of the Urakami Christians—the so-called "Fourth Collapse."

瓦礫の奥に仮聖堂と南側壁。

The southern wall and temporary church are visible beyond the rubble.

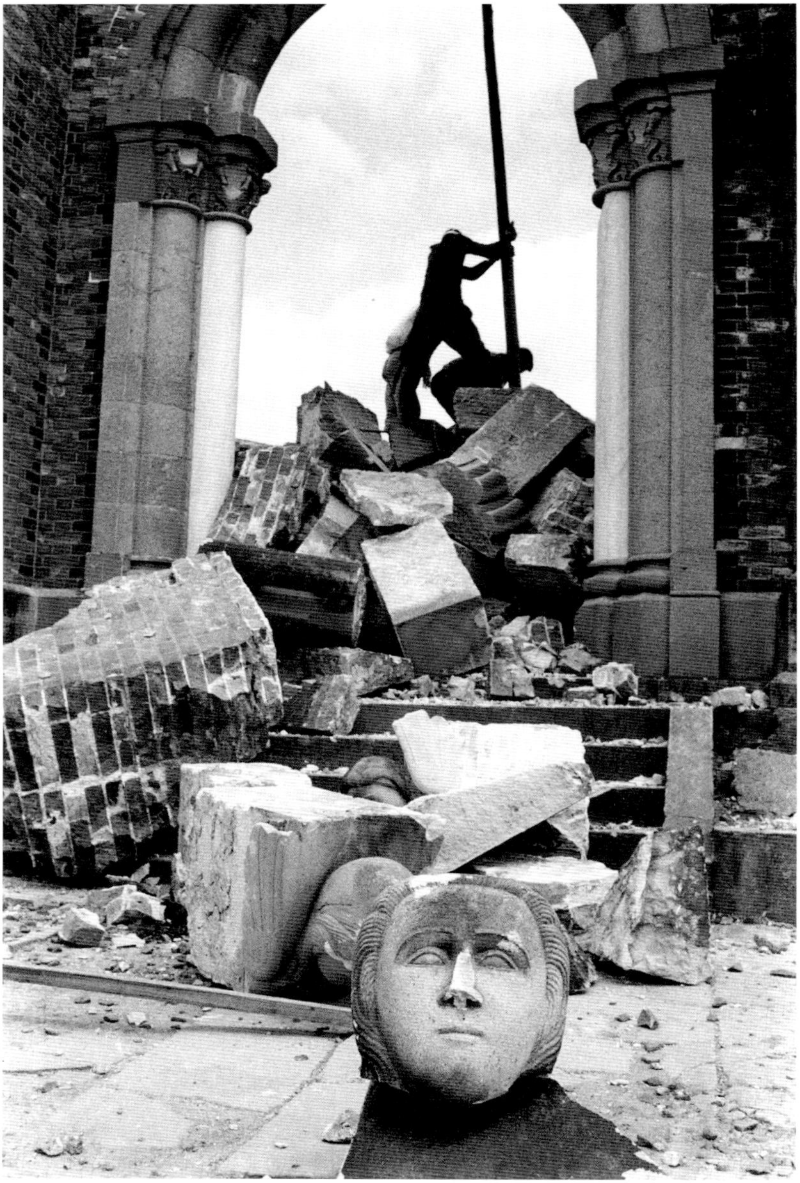

頭部と手足を失った「十字架上のキリスト像」。「復活後のキリスト像」の頭部が添えられている。奥に天使像。浦上の人びと同様、全身に放射能をあび、熱線に焼かれ、爆風に吹き飛ばされ、そして浦上の阿鼻叫喚を見つめた。

Only the torso of this statue of Christ on the Cross remains. A head of the "Resurrected Savior" and images of angels are lined up in the rear. Like the people of Urakami, these artifacts were showered with radiation, burned by the flash of heat, scattered by the blast, and left to gaze at the atomic wasteland.

地上に横たわる「悲しみの聖母像」。黒い影が痛ましい。

The statue of Mary in Mourning lies on the ground, discolored and disfigured.

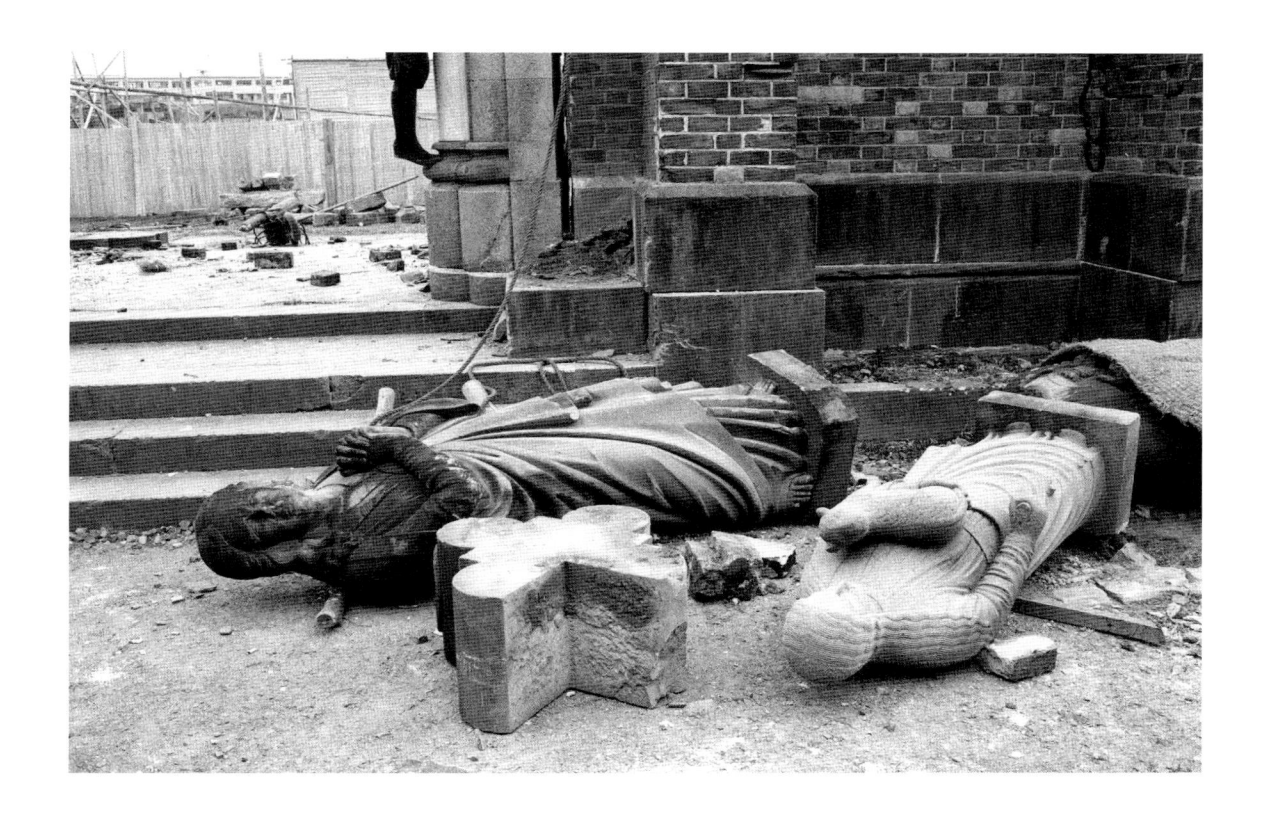

南側壁。左が「使徒聖ヨハネ像」、右は「聖アグネス像」。

The statues of St. John the Apostle and St. Agnes lie to the left and right, near the southern wall.

「使徒聖ヨハネ像」。胸元に作業靴のゴム底の跡がある。

Statue of St. John the Apostle. The footprint from a work shoe is visible on the chest.

運搬用ロープを巻かれた「使徒聖ヨハネ像」。

Statue of St. John the Apostle, tied up with rope for transport.

持ち運ばれる天使半身像。

The bust of an angel is hoisted onto a stretcher.

運び出される「使徒聖ヨハネ像」。現在の天主堂の正面入口に置かれている。

The statue of St. John the Apostle is carried away. Today, it is installed outside the arched portal at the front of the new cathedral.

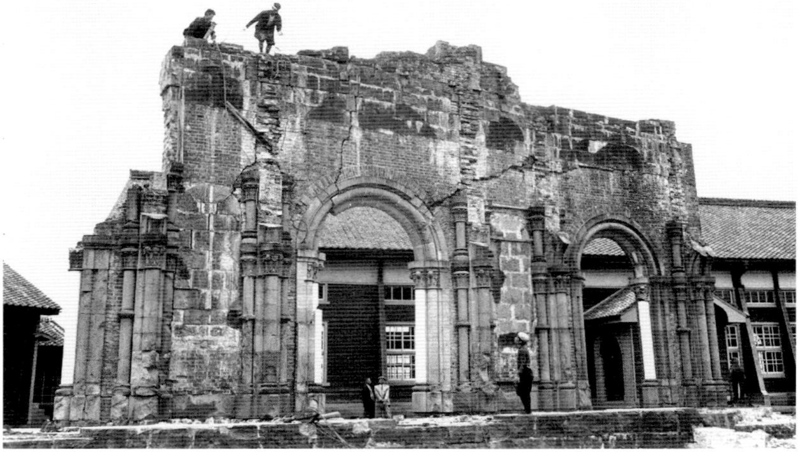

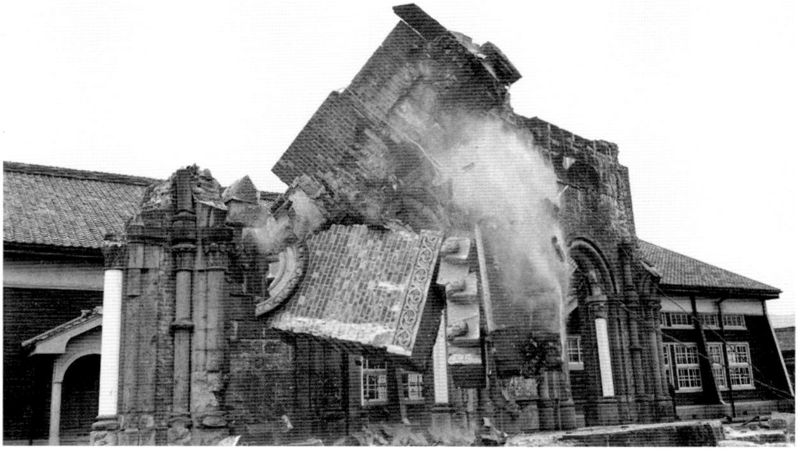

倒される南側壁。背後に見えるのは仮聖堂。

The southern wall is pulled down. The temporary church stands in the background.

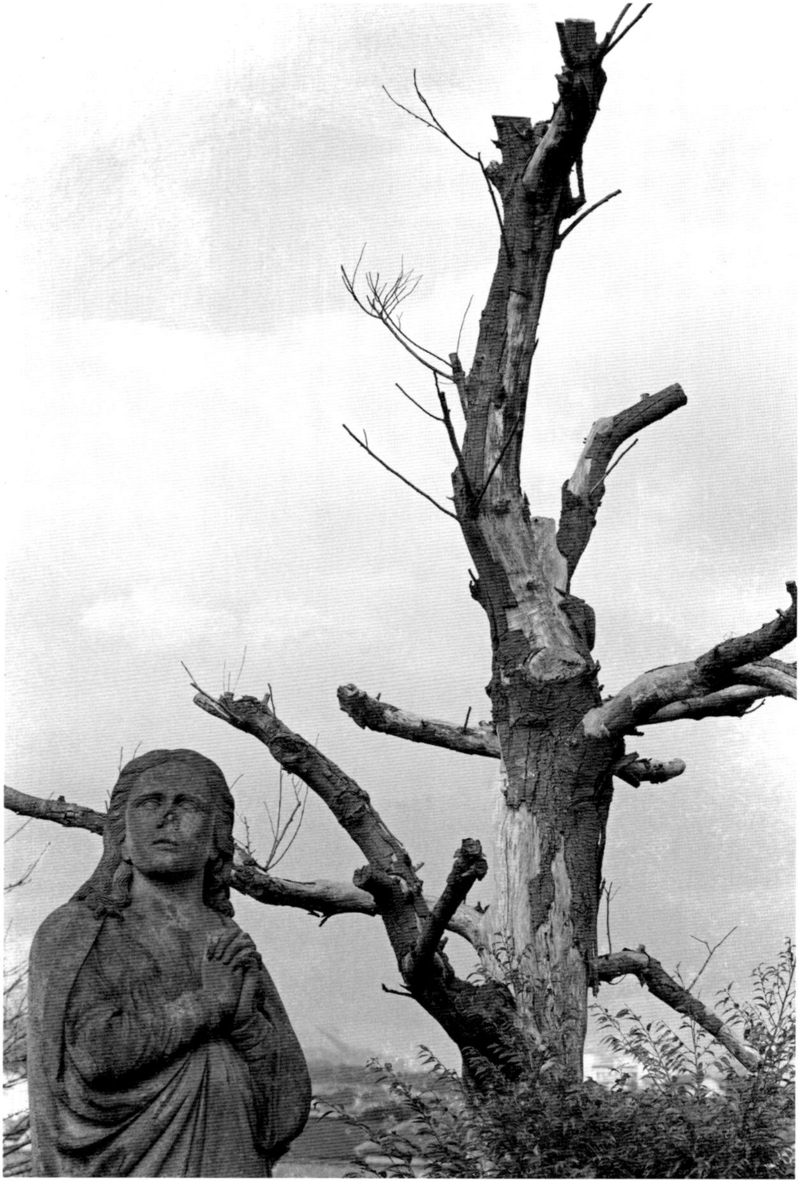

1958年3月に着工、翌年10月に完成した新浦上天主堂。建坪509坪、塔の高さ29㍍、ロマネスク様式と近代建築を組み合わせた鉄筋コンクリート造。正面外壁には、中央の新たな「十字架上のキリスト像」の両脇に、フレノ神父が彫刻した小型の「悲しみの聖母」「使徒聖ヨハネ」両被爆像を掲げ、旧天主堂の面影を残した。1960年撮影。

The new Urakami Cathedral reached completion in October 1959 after 19 months of work, a ferroconcrete structure combining Romanesque architecture and modern styles, with a floor space of 509 *tsubo* (about 1,679 square meters) and belfries rising to a height of 29 meters. The statue of Christ on the Cross installed at the front was new, but it was flanked by small statues of Mary in Mourning and St. John the Apostle carved by Fr. Pierre-Théodore Fraineau and exposed to the atomic bombing. Takahara Itaru took this photograph in 1960.

解　説

横 手 一 彦

近世の浦上

　長崎市北部に位置する浦上は、かつて長崎の港に近い一寒村に過ぎなかった。深く湾入する遠浅の海は、現在平和公園のある丘陵地の裾野のあたりにまで、穏やかな波を寄せていた。この一帯は20世紀初頭に長崎港を浚渫した土砂で埋め立てられたが、浦上の地名は、この〈浦〉の〈上〉に位置する村であったことに由来する。

　1549年、フランシスコ・ザビエルが鹿児島に上陸し、日本にキリスト教が伝えられた。当時長崎の領主であった大村純忠は、大名として初めて洗礼を受け、宣教師を厚遇し、領民を改宗させた。長崎は、ポルトガル船の入港地として開港され、1580年にはイエズス会に寄進された。以後の長崎は、貿易と布教が一体化して流入し、東西の文化が交差する地として華やいだ。

　当時有馬晴信の領地だった浦上も、1584年にイエズス会に寄進され、神父や修道士が生活を共にし、村人を司牧する地となった。1605年、肥後の豪族であった菊地蒲三郎正重が、浦上山里村の世襲庄屋に任じられた。名を高谷小左衛門と改め、浦上の小高い丘──後に浦上天主堂が建てられた場所──に屋敷を構え、村の長となった。

　しかし1612年、徳川家康は幕府直轄地をキリスト教禁制とし、翌々年には全国にも同様の触れを出した。長崎でも宣教師（バテレン）は追放され、浦上山里村のサンタ・クララ教会などの聖堂が破壊された。そしてオランダと清国以外の交易を禁じる鎖国の時代が到来する。

　長崎の街には、仏教諸宗派の僧侶が招かれ、大音寺や興福寺などの大寺が建立された。1625年には諏訪神社が再興され、やがて盛大な神事が行われるようになる。今に続く秋の大祭「長崎くんち」である。「諏訪神事は、吉利支丹の伝播を防ぐにも、最もいゝ方法であつた、幕府は特に、その祭礼の当日には、長崎奉行を参拝させ、尚御輿の御供を命じたのであつた」（永見徳太郎『南蛮長崎草』1926年、春陽堂）。キリスト教の街は、仏教徒と神社氏子の街へと変わった。

　浦上の数千の信徒は、檀那寺である聖徳寺で宗門改めを受け（寺請制度）、正月14日と15日に庄屋宅で踏絵を強制された。聖像を踏むことが出来ず、信仰への忠誠心が露見すれば、庭木に縛り付けられ、「転び」（改宗）を強いる拷問が行われた。絵を踏むことで難を得ずに帰宅した信徒は、自らの足を洗い、その水を飲み干し、許しを請う気持ちを祈りに込めた。近世の浦上山里村を舞台に「転び」を扱った作品として、芥川龍之介の「おぎん」（『中央公論』1922年9月）がある。火あぶりにされる直前、孝行心から棄教する童女を主人公に、受難史のなかで「最も恥づべき躓きとして、後代に伝へられた物語」の裏にあった葛藤を描いている。

　信徒たちは禁教下において、表向きは仏教を受け入れたが、幕府の監視をすり抜けて密かな宗門組織をつくった。この組織は、「帳方」と呼ばれる指導者が、宗教暦を管理して行事日を定め、教理を伝承する役割を担った。「水方」は、洗礼を授与する役割を負い、1郷に1名、計4名で構成された。「聞役」は、宗教行事などの重要事項を密かに伝えるなどの個別的な指導を担い、1郷に数名がその任にあたった。この指揮系統による秘密組織が互いを支え、父祖が伝える教えを守った。浦上は、初代孫右衛門から7代吉蔵が殉教するまで、「帳方」7世代、250年にわたり、教会や聖像を失ったまま密かな信仰を受け継ぐ潜伏キリシタンの村であった。

近代の浦上

　それでも、密告や密偵によって、潜伏キリシタンの存在が発覚することがあった。発覚と捕縛は、「崩れ」と呼ばれた。浦上の潜伏キリシタンは幕末まで、1790年、

Commentary

Yokote Kazuhiko

Urakami in the Edo Period

Urakami was a tiny farming hamlet hidden in hills to the north of the international port of Nagasaki, where a shallow inlet stretched up to the area that today is Peace Park. In the early 20th century the upper part of the inlet was filled in with earth and sand dredged from Nagasaki Harbor, but the name Urakami, which literally means "head of the bay," continues to describe the original geography.

In 1549, St. Francis Xavier came ashore at Kagoshima and began the promulgation of Christianity. Omura Sumitada, in whose domain Nagasaki was located at the time, became the first feudal lord to receive baptism, to welcome the European missionaries, and to urge his subjects to embrace Christianity. Omura not only opened Nagasaki as a port for the Portuguese trade in 1570 but even ceded it to the Society of Jesus a decade later, helping the town to flourish as a base for trade and missionary activity and an intersection for the cultures of East and West.

In 1584, the hamlet of Urakami, part of the domain of feudal lord Arima Harunobu, was also ceded to the Society of Jesus and turned into a site of contact between villagers and missionaries. In 1605, a wealthy resident of Higo (modern-day Kumamoto Prefecture) named Kikuchi Kamasaburo Masashige was appointed to the post of hereditary village headman at Urakami-Yamazato and took the name Takatani Kozaemon, establishing his residence on the low hill that would later become the site of Urakami Cathedral.

Drastic changes occurred in 1612. Shogun Tokugawa Ieyasu enforced a ban on Christianity in the districts under jurisdiction of the *bakufu* government (Shogunate) and extended it throughout Japan two years later. This meant the expulsion of European missionaries and the destruction of all Christian facilities including the Church of Santa Clara in the village of Urakami-Yamazato. The Tokugawa Shogunate restricted foreign trade to the Dutch and Chinese in Nagasaki and imposed a strict policy of national isolation.

Buddhist and Shinto priests arrived to fill the vacuum in Nagasaki. Daionji, Kofukuji and other large Buddhist temples were erected, and in 1625 Suwa Shinto Shrine was revived as a spiritual and social refuge for the people of the city. The autumn festival "Nagasaki Kunchi," which continues to this day, was launched at the shrine around this time. In his book *Namban Nagasaki Kusa* (Tales of Christian Nagasaki), Nagami Tokutaro comments that, "The Shogunate considered the festivities of Suwa Shinto Shrine an excellent way to prevent the spread of Christianity, and, on the day of the festival, its magistrates in Nagasaki were compelled to pray at the shrine and to provide the holy palanquins." (Shunyodo, 1926) In a matter of a few years, Nagasaki changed from a Christian enclave into the home of Buddhist and Shinto followers.

The several thousand Christian villagers of Urakami, meanwhile, were forced like all other Japanese to become parishioners of a Buddhist temple, which in their case was the nearby Shotokuji. In addition, they were required every year on January 14 and 15 to visit the house of the village headman and to step on a Christian image (a custom called *fumie*, or "trampling the picture") as proof of renunciation. If a person refused to comply, he or she would be tied to a tree in the garden and tortured until finally relenting. The people who avoided this grim fate by complying would go home, wash their feet, and pray for forgiveness by drinking the wash water. Among the literary works dealing with this sad chapter of history is the novel *Ogin* by Japanese author Akutagawa Ryunosuke (Chuokoronsha, 1922) which depicts the terrible dilemma of a young woman named Ogin who, although willing to face a martyr's death by burning at the stake, recants at the last moment in order to save her par-

1842年、1856年の3度の「崩れ」を経験した。そして江戸幕府瓦解直前の1867年7月に、最後にして最大のキリシタン弾圧「浦上四番崩れ」が起こる。

　発端は、1864年の大浦天主堂の建立であった。19世紀半ば、江戸幕府は米国の圧力をきっかけに開国を受け入れ、安政五ヵ国条約を結んだ。これにより、特定の地に外国人居留地が置かれ、商業や治外法権が認められた。幕府は居留地における教会の設置も認めざるをえなかったが、国内のキリスト教禁制はそのままであった。長崎では1862年、アメリカ人宣教師が東山手にプロテスタント教会を建てたのに引き続き、その3年後、パリ外国宣教会の宣教師が長崎南山手乙1番地にカトリック教会を建設する。翌年、浦上の村人は、この教会──大浦天主堂を訪れ、見物人にまぎれて小祭壇のサンタ・マリア像を見上げた。そして、この「フランス寺」と呼ばれる建物に住む異人こそが、禁教下の250年、その再来が密かに伝えられ、持ち焦がれた「パーテル様」（司祭）であることを知った。数日後の3月17日、浦上の潜伏キリシタンは大浦天主堂を訪れ、自分たちが密かに守り続けた信仰を告白し、後に長崎の初代司教となるプチジャン神父の教化を受けた。ローマ・カトリック教会はこれを「信徒発見」「キリシタン復活」と呼び、宗教史に特筆される出来事とする。

　浦上の信徒は、村内に4ヵ所の秘密礼拝堂を建て、そこを宣教師が巡回し、洗礼を授け、教理を教えた。そしてついに彼らは、葬儀の仕方を巡って檀那寺と対立し、その関わりを絶つことを決意した。寺請制度を拒否したのである。浦上が、潜伏キリシタンの里であることが公然となるに至り、1867年7月、村の主だった男女68名が捕縛され、拷問を受けた。この迫害が、「浦上四番崩れ」の始まりである。

　ほどなく江戸幕府は倒れたが、明治新政府は禁教令を引き継ぎ、その後1870年、さらに浦上山里村の男女老幼3394名が流罪に処せられた。彼らは、名古屋以西の石高10万石以上の20藩の預かりとなり、各藩主に生殺与奪の権が与えられた。浦上の信徒は、これを「旅」と呼んだ。浦上山里村の総戸数約1000戸のうち、仏教徒を除く約800戸が「旅」に出、空き家の家財類は直ぐさま略奪されたといわれる。一帯は、ほぼ無人の村となった。いくつかの藩では、棄教を強制する厳しい拷問が行われ、613名が流配地において殉教し、1011名が棄教した。

　長崎に在留する各国の領事や英字新聞 Nagasaki Express の記者がこれを伝えたことから、列強の在日代表者は日本政府のキリシタン弾圧に激しく抗議した。これは海外の新聞でも取り上げられ、国際問題に発展する。1871年から欧米外遊に出た岩倉使節団は、各国でこれに対する非難を受けた。こうした事態を重く受け止めた新政府は、1873年、ついに禁教の高札を撤去したのである。

　長い「旅」は終わり、信徒が浦上の地に帰ることを許された時、帰ることができたのは、およそ1900名に減っていた。住む家のない者のために、村内の35ヵ所に掘立小屋が建てられた。着替えも布団もなく、荒れた畑を陶片で掘り起こし、虫のついた切り干し芋や醤油滓を常食とした。この貧窮に、赤痢などの人災や台風などの天災が重なった。細農が多く、また狭小な田畑では、日々の暮らしを満たすことが出来なかったが、小作や小商い、日雇いなどで日々の糧を得て、オラショ（祈り）を捧げながら、極貧のなかから村の再建に努めたのである。

　明治の始め、この地の世襲庄屋の当主高谷官十郎が死亡し、残された家族は生活に困窮して居宅地を手放し、村を立ち退いた。1880年6月に浦上の信徒は、この庄屋屋敷を1600円（当時米1俵2円64銭）で購入し、家屋を改修して仮聖堂とした。長い禁教の時代に踏絵が行われ、仕置きを受けた悲しみの屋敷が、「神の家」となったのである。

　1895年、信徒5千人の総意で本聖堂の建設を決した。フレノ神父の設計により、ロマネスクを模したアーチ形玄関、イオニア風白大理石円柱、赤煉瓦側面、クポラ（円天井）を備える壮大な聖堂建設が始まった。信徒たちは、決して豊かではない生活から資金を献じた。浦上の古老の話によれば、「街へ筍や野菜売りに出掛け、その代金で帰途に煉瓦を買ったりしたと父から聞かされた」という。彼らは、石塊を刻み、労働も供して「神の家」の建設に勤しんだ。汗と涙と祈りが込められた天主堂の

ents from grief and fulfill her filial responsibility as a Japanese.

During the long period of persecution, the villagers pretended to embrace Buddhism but formed secret underground cells to practice their Christian faith. Each cell had a leader, called *chōkata*, who administrated the religious calendar, set dates for ceremonies, and managed the transmission of Christian tenets. Another person, called *mizukata*, officiated at baptisms. There was one *mizukata* in each hamlet or a total of four. Several people in each hamlet also assumed the role of *kikiyaku*, or "listeners," conducting personal instruction and secretly informing other villagers about religious matters. The members of these secret organizations supported and encouraged each other and maintained the faith of their forebears with unwavering fidelity. Urakami, where the *chōkata* did their duty for seven generations from Magoemon to the martyr Kichizo, was a village of underground Christians who kept the secret light of faith aglow for two and a half centuries without a church, without religious figures, and without any contact with priests.

Urakami in Modern History

Informants and spies occasionally betrayed the presence of the underground Christian cells. The discovery of cells and the persecutions that followed were referred to as *kuzure* or "collapse." The Urakami villagers experienced a collapse on three occasions in 1790, 1842 and 1856. Then in July 1867, only a few months before the demise of the Tokugawa Shogunate, the greatest setback of all gained a permanent niche in history: the *yonban kuzure* or "Fourth Collapse."

The origin of the affair was the construction of Oura Catholic Church in the Nagasaki Foreign Settlement in 1864. The Tokugawa Shogunate had bent to foreign pressure the previous decade and signed the Ansei Five-Power Treaty in 1858, agreeing to the establishment of designated districts where foreigners could engage in commercial activities and enjoy extraterritorial rights. As a result the Japanese had no choice but to permit the construction of churches in the foreign settlements, even though this concession contradicted the ban on Christianity still in effect among the Japanese populace. In 1862, American missionaries established a Protestant church in the Higashiyamate neighborhood of the Nagasaki Foreign Settlement, and this was followed two years later by a Catholic church built at No.1A Minamiyamate by missionaries from the Société des Mission Etrangères de Paris (Paris Foreign Missions Society). Urakami villagers visited the site and mixed with other spectators ogling the "French Temple" and its strange accouterments, and it did not take them long to realize that the French priests were of the same cut as the priests of legend who brought news of Christianity to Japan 250 years earlier. On March 17, 1865, a few of the villagers revealed their faith to Fr. Bernard Petitjean, an event that marked the discovery of the ancient underground Christians of Japan and a focal point in Christian history.

The French priests visited the four secret shrines erected by villagers in Urakami, conducted baptisms and taught catechism. Some time later the villagers, who disagreed with the Buddhist priests at Shotokuji over the manner of conducting a funeral, defied the temple registration system (*terauke seido*) in force since the 17th century, publicly revealing Urakami as a Christian village. The result was the arrest and torture of 68 people in July 1867 and the beginning of the "Fourth Collapse."

The Tokugawa Shogunate soon ceased to exist, but the new Meiji government upheld the ban on Christianity and in 1870 arrested a total of 3,394 people of all ages from the Urakami-Yamazato district, exiled them to 20 prominent domains in western Japan, and left their fate to the discretion of the leader of each domain. The people of Urakami refer to this event in retrospect as *tabi*, or the "journey." Of the approximately 1,000 households in the Urakami-Yamazato district at the time, excluding people of Buddhist faith, some 800 families were compelled to embark on this tragic excursion and leave their homes and belongings prone to looters. As a result, Urakami was reduced to a virtual ghost town. In the sites of exile, meanwhile, 613 people succumbed to torture and another 1,011 recanted.

The foreign consuls in Nagasaki and the writer of reports in the English-language newspaper *Nagasaki Express* alerted the representatives of foreign powers in Japan and triggered a flurry of protests to the Japa-

赤煉瓦一片いっぺんが、長い歳月をかけて積まれた。フレノ神父が、この道の半ばで過労に斃れ、事業は後任のラゲ神父（新約聖書邦訳者）に引き継がれた。1920年10月に、浦上山里村は長崎市に編入された。

1914年、ついに天主堂は献堂式をあげ、1925年には双塔の鐘楼が完成した。鐘楼には、フランス製の小鐘と大鐘が吊るされた。長い迫害に耐え、「旅」から帰り、信仰を守り続け、信仰の力を30年積み重ねた浦上の丘に、東洋一といわれる荘厳な大聖堂が完成したのである。

> すつくと眼前に立ちはだかつた感じのするこの天主堂の角と言ふ角にはキリストやマリヤの像が刻みつけられて異国情緒的な臭を発散して居ります。中はがらんとして広く正面には一段と美しく彫刻された祭壇――ミサと言ふ事を行ふ所でせうか――があつて侵しがたい何物かがある様な気にもなつて見ました（島尾敏雄「浦上天主堂印象」『峠』1934年9月）。

> たうとう僕の眼は、浦上の天主堂が丘の上に、ちひさい花のやうに赤く建つてゐるのを見た（立原道造「長崎紀行」1938年12月4日）。

長崎は、近代以降もその地勢的な位置から大陸への窓口としてあり、造船業や鉱業に加えて兵器生産などの軍需産業に支えられた都市であった。満州事変が勃発した1931年に、長崎市大浦の香港上海銀行が閉鎖される。そして日本が長く暗い戦争への道を歩み始めると、他の都市にまして、国策の直接的な影響を受けた。

日中戦争が始まった1937年2月、邦人初の長崎司教早坂久之助が病気辞職し、その後に浦上出身の山口愛次郎が任命される。パウロ山口愛次郎は、ローマのウルバノ大学に学び、天主堂が完成した1925年に帰国した。翌年に長崎公教神学校教授となり、1936年から鹿児島教区長として赴任した。日本のキリスト信徒は、次第に日本人の高位聖職者によって指導されるようになったのである。その後に山口愛次郎司教は、宣撫要員として戦地に派遣された。

1940年、戦艦武蔵が長崎の三菱造船所で建造された。翌1941年12月、日米開戦。真珠湾攻撃で攻撃機に搭載された魚雷は、長崎の兵器工場で生産されたといわれる。1943年10月に長崎市内で、防空壕堀が始まった。戦時末期に天主堂は、食糧倉庫として米3千俵や煮干千袋を備蓄した。司祭も、村人も、そして天主堂も、世界戦争を戦うことを求められたのである。

被爆地浦上

日本の敗色が濃厚となっていた1945年7月、米軍が原爆投下の目標とした都市は、広島、小倉、新潟のほか、京都が日本の古都であるという理由で除外され、そのかわりに長崎がリストに加えられた。そして最初の核兵器による破壊は、8月6日の朝、広島市で起こった。原爆は作戦通りに、目標地点とされた市内の中心部を流れる太田川に掛かる相生橋に投下されたのである。

二つ目の原爆は、9日の朝、小倉に投下される予定であった。原爆投下に際し、機上の爆撃手には、目標地点の目視確認が厳命されていた。しかし小倉上空には、前日に爆撃された八幡製鉄所の硝煙や靄などが立ち籠め、目標地点とされた小倉造兵廠を遮蔽していた。加えて、離陸直前に予備燃料ポンプが故障するトラブルもあり、帰途の燃料不足が懸念された。3度試みても目視確認は出来ず、作戦は第2目標都市の長崎市に変更され、搭載機はすぐに長崎市へ向かった。

目標地点は、長崎市中心部を流れる中島川に掛かる常盤橋付近。主要な兵器工場と市街地の壊滅が目的とされたのである。長崎市上空に飛来した搭載機が、雲塊の切れ目から目視確認した地点は、しかし、目標地点からやや外れ、9日午前11時2分、プルトニウム型原爆「ファットマン」が、上空約9600メートルから投下され、長崎市松山町171番地の地上500メートルで炸裂した。

そこは、市北部浦上地区の、軍需工場と住宅が密集する地域であった。巨大なエネルギーは太陽光線を遮り、一瞬周囲は暗黒となった。次の瞬間、それは地上の物体を粉砕し、吹き飛ばし、上空に吸い上げ、突き落とし、火の玉の雨を四方に降らせた。浦上は火炎に包まれた。

この時、浦上天主堂では8月15日の「聖母被昇天の日」に向けた準備が進められ、主任司祭西田三郎が天主

nese government over its anti-Christian actions. The news was also picked up by newspapers abroad and grew into an international issue. During their tour of Western countries in 1871, the members of the Iwakura Delegation met with protests and castigation at each stop along the way. The new Meiji government, disturbed by this global reaction, finally withdrew the ban on Christianity in 1873.

By the time they were able to return to their homes, the Urakami villagers were reduced in number to about 1,900. Makeshift shelters were erected in 35 locations in the Urakami-Yamazato district for the homeless. Bereft of clothing, bedding and tools, the villagers used scraps of broken pottery to till their neglected farmland and kept starvation at bay with bug-bitten potatoes and soy sauce dregs. This severe destitution was exacerbated by attacks of dysentery and the damaging effects of typhoons and other natural disasters. The thin strips of farmland at their disposal were utterly insufficient, but the villagers eked out a living by engaging in day labor for other farmers and small-scale merchants, all the while keeping their spirits high with prayer and striving to rebuild their beautiful village.

In the early Meiji Period, the last hereditary village headman Takatani Kanjuro died, and his family, left to poverty, abandoned the house in Urakami and went elsewhere. In June 1880, the Urakami Christians purchased the property for 1,600 yen (an enormous sum of money at a time when a bushel of rice cost only 2.64 yen) and converted the house into a temporary church. The house of sadness where the villagers and their descendants had endured torture and the humiliation of *fumie* was now a "House of God."

In 1895, the approximately 5,000 Christians of Urakami decided unanimously to construct a full-fledged cathedral. The French priest Pierre-Théodore Fraineau drew up plans for a building of Romanesque design with arched portals, Ionian pillars of white marble, brick walls, and a grand sanctuary capped with a classical cupola. The parishioners squeezed donations from their scant savings. One elderly resident remembered hearing that her father had gone into town to sell bamboo sprouts and vegetables and, with the money thus earned, purchased bricks on the way home.

These people selflessly offered their labor in carving stones and constructing the church building and piled one sweat-stained brick on top of another to make the walls. Fr. Fraineau died before seeing the completion of the building and was succeeded by Fr. Emile Raguet, a Belgian missionary known for his work in translating the New Testament into Japanese. In October 1920, the village of Urakami-Yamazato was absorbed into Nagasaki City.

In 1914, the cathedral was inaugurated in an official ceremony, but it was not until 1925 that the twin belfries finally reached completion. One large and another small bell cast in France were installed in the belfries. Hailed as the grandest church in the Orient, Urakami Cathedral rose not only from the Nagasaki skyline but also from the long period of persecution and endurance, the "journey" and its untold hardships, and the accumulation of 30 years of love and labor inspired by unbending religious faith.

The church seemed to loom up in front of me, carved on every corner and every niche with statues of Christ and Mary and exuding the exotic aroma of faraway lands. The interior was huge and empty, a wide altar with more splendid sculptures rising in the recesses—presumably the place where the ceremony called 'Mass' is conducted. As I looked I felt the presence of something indefinable and impenetrable.
(Shimao Toshio, "Urakami Tenshudō Inshō" [Impressions of Urakami Cathedral] in *Tōge*, September 1934)

Finally my eyes rose to the top of the hill where the cathedral of Urakami was standing, red like a lovely flower.
(Tachihara Michizo, *Nagasaki Kikō* [Nagasaki Travelogue], December 4, 1938)

Nagasaki has served from the beginning of modern history as Japan's closest port to China and a gateway to the continent. In addition to traditional industries like shipbuilding and mining, the urban economy of the early 20th century began to rely on the manufacture of munitions. In 1931, the same year as the Manchurian

堂に向かう途中にあり、助任司祭玉屋房吉は天主堂内の告解場で信徒24名とともにいた。司祭と信徒は、天主堂と運命を共にし、1人の生存者もなかった。天主堂は、軍の備蓄米などが燃える青い炎に揺らぎ続けた。浦上信徒1万2千名のうち8500名の命が一瞬のうちに奪われたといわれる。また長崎の原爆による死傷者約14万人のうち、兵役や軍務に適合する世代の男性の数は千名余りと推定される。死傷者のほとんどは、子どもや女性や老人などの非戦闘員であった。

その夜、天空には三日月が昇った。翌日は、油照りの一日であった。瀕死の被爆者や黒焦げとなった焼死体。公園や校庭や広場は、火葬場に変わった。

1945年8月15日、日本はポツダム宣言を受諾し、2度目の世界戦争に敗北した。この知らせに、世界中の人びとが歓喜した。

> 貧苦のドン底に突落された運命の下に、先ず我鬼道生活から始まり、雨露を凌ぐ家とは名ばかりのわび住居を建て、焼野と化した荒地を開墾し、只管に余命を全うせんとキューキューとして、数限り無き苦労を続けて来た。(中略)静かに過去を顧みるに、世界平和の確立という美名の下に戦線と銃後の完全一致にもかかわらず協力に依り、負わされたる戦争の犠牲は如何に大であつたか、此の歩み来た総ては、かんなん辛苦の道の連続であつた(深堀達雄「試練」『荒野』2号、1947年11月、浦上カトリック連合青年会)

浦上の人びとは、家財や家族、知友を失い、地獄の臭いが漂う谷底に沈み込んだ。しかし一木一草もない灰色の地に焼けトタンの小屋を建て、被爆後の地べたに生きる手立てを探し求めた。

> 双塔の昔の姿今なけれ　斜陽の御堂　げに尊かり
> （山里小学校長土井良井『荒野』2号）

天主堂は、廃墟となった。後に聖フランシスコ病院となる浦上第一病院の一部が焼け残り、生き残った信徒はその1階の修道士食堂20坪の窓枠にむしろを吊って仮の聖堂とし、そこに集った。この年の11月23日、原爆犠牲者合同慰霊祭が、廃墟となった天主堂で開かれ、被爆後に初めて浦上信徒が一堂に会した。浦上出身の浦川和三郎司祭は、生き残った信徒600名を前に、生前の信徒の名をあげながら、追悼の説教を行った。

> そして浦上はこのような焼野原になりました。明治6年に「旅」から帰って来た時は、「あばら屋」でしたが、浦上に家が残っていましたが、今は一軒の家もありません

この言葉に、参列者はみな号泣する。何も、なかった。しかし、再びここから立ち上がる他に、生きる方途はどこにもなかったのである。

浦上に限らず、原爆直下をかろうじて生き延びた被爆者は、総てを失った生活苦、寄る辺ない毎日、病を抱えた身、近親者を失った孤独、その後の社会的な蔑視などから——定かではなく、確かめようもない数字でもあるが——直接被爆者の4人に1人ほどの割合で、自らの命を絶ったといわれる。被爆後も、死の恐怖がおそった。被爆者の途方もない困難、受忍限度を越えた痛みや苦しみのなかで、人として生き、そして死ぬということが、もはや普通のことではあり得なかった。そのような現実を、彼らは生きたのである。

残留放射能によって、70年間は草木も生えないと噂された。しかし被爆から1ヵ月ほどすると、大地に草が芽吹いた。人びとは、自然から生きる力を与えられたように感じ、空き地に野菜の種を蒔き始めた。

天主堂の鐘楼の小鐘は大破したが、大鐘は崩壊した瓦礫から掘り出された。これが杉丸太で組まれた仮鐘楼に吊され、1945年12月24日の夜、被爆後初めて浦上の谷に鳴り響いた。信徒は、喜びに震えながら「長崎の鐘」に耳を傾けた。その胸には万感の思いが突き上げ、その悲しみは尽きることはなかった。翌年12月に仮鐘楼は、鉄骨に造り替えられる。

> 倒れたる墓標に孤児合掌す　（森内秀雄「風詩」『荒野』2号）

Incident and the closing of the Nagasaki branch of the Hong Kong and Shanghai Bank, Japan began its long march down the dark path to war, its national policies affecting Nagasaki even more deeply than other cities around the country.

With the outbreak of war between Japan and China in February 1937, Hayasaka Kyunosuke, the first Japanese bishop of Nagasaki, retired in poor health and was replaced by Yamaguchi Aijiro, a native of Urakami village. Yamaguchi, whose baptismal name was Paul, had studied at the Pontifical University in Rome and returned to Japan in 1925, the same year that Urakami Cathedral reached completion. The following year he assumed the post of professor at the Nagasaki Catholic Divinity School and in 1936 went to Kagoshima to head the diocese there. These achievements marked the beginning of a change from French to Japanese leadership in the Catholic community. The bishop of Nagasaki would soon be sent to the battlefields to engage in pacification work.

In 1940, the giant battleship *Musashi* reached completion at the Mitsubishi Nagasaki Shipyard, and in December the following year war broke out between Japan and the United States. It is said that the torpedoes used in the attack on Pearl Harbor were made in the munitions factories at Nagasaki. In October 1943, the people of Nagasaki began to dig cave shelters in preparation for the air raids already pounding other Japanese cities. In the closing months of the war, Urakami Cathedral was converted into a warehouse for the storage of food stuffs. Everything and everyone including the priests, the Catholic faithful and the holy church were made to participate in the fighting of a world war.

Urakami, the Site of an Atomic Bombing

In July 1945, with Japan's disadvantage in the war already painfully clear, the American armed forces selected several Japanese cities as targets for the use of atomic bombs. Although included at first along with Hiroshima, Kokura and Niigata, Kyoto was dropped from the list because of its status as Japan's ancient capital. The city chosen to replace it was Nagasaki. On August 6, Hiroshima became the first human habitation in the world subjected to destruction by a nuclear weapon.

The mission proceeded exactly as planned, the atomic bomb exploding in the sky over Aioi Bridge and Ota River in the heart of the Hiroshima urban area.

On the morning of August 9, an aircraft carrying the second atomic bomb flew to the industrial city of Kokura in northern Kyushu. The bombardier was under strict orders to release the bomb only after visual confirmation of the target, but he found the targeting point—the Kokura Arms Factory—shrouded with mist and smoke from an air raid conducted on the Yahata Steel Works the previous day. This predicament was aggravated by a possible fuel shortage due to the failure of a reserve fuel pump, which had been discovered just before take-off. Three attempts at visual confirmation proved futile, and the captain ordered his crew to fly to the reserve target, Nagasaki.

The targeting point, Tokiwa Bridge spanning Nakashima River in the center of Nagasaki, had been selected to assure the destruction of major munitions factories and the obliteration of the city. However, the bombardier failed to pinpoint the target and released his deadly cargo off-target after catching a glimpse of the city through a break in the clouds. The plutonium-core atomic bomb, nicknamed "Fat Man," plummeted from an altitude of 9,600 meters and exploded about 500 meters in the sky over No. 171 Matsuyama-machi. It was 11:02 a.m., August 9, 1945.

Matsuyama-machi was part of the Urakami district, a tight-knit mesh of munitions factories and residential neighborhoods. The gigantic burst of energy generated by the explosion veiled the sun and threw the city into darkness, then, an instant later, crushed everything on the face of the earth to pieces, yanked the debris up into the sky, hurled pellets of fire in all directions, and turned the Urakami district into a hellish conflagration.

Preparations had been underway at Urakami Cathedral for the celebration of the Assumption of the Virgin Mary on August 15. The rector, Fr. Nishida Saburo, had been on his way to the church, while his assistant, Fr. Tamaya Fusayoshi, had been in the building hearing confessions. None of the priests or 24 parishioners in the church survived. The rice and foodstuffs stored in the devastated building meanwhile emitted strange blue flames. An estimated 8,500 of the 12,000

南瓜の茎や種も、炒って食べた。薩摩芋と南瓜の煮付けが御馳走であった。そのような生活のなかでも、浦上の信仰の火は絶えることがなかった。やがて復員軍人や引揚者などで信徒が増え、仮の聖堂が手狭となった。1946年11月、信徒は山に登って木を切り出し、廃墟の天主堂の横に、171坪の新たな仮の聖堂を作った。1948年5月には公民館も建て、その2階の一部は司祭館に転用された。

　日本は、他国の軍隊が占領する国となった。未だかつて、日本の歴史になかったことである。連合国軍最高司令官総司令部（GHQ）が日本全土を軍事占領し、沖縄を除く46都道府県に地方組織としての軍政部を置いた。長崎軍政部は長崎税関ビルに置かれ、武装解除と住民監視を主な軍務とし、銃剣類の没収を行った。この間接統治は、1950年1月まで続く。

　原爆が投下されてから2ヵ月が経った10月8日付の「長崎新聞」は、二つの祭事の模様を伝えている。

　　絢爛偲ぶ奉納踊り／"お宮日"の幕ひらく
　　焼跡の広場に"ミサ"／壕生活の信徒一千

　前者は、中島川沿いの住民たちによる「長崎くんち」の奉納踊りである。戦時中に途絶えていた諏訪神社の秋の大祭が、部分的にではあったが、敗戦のこの年に執り行われた。これと対照的に、後者は爆心地浦上の模様を伝えている。先に触れた11月の合同慰霊祭の前に、死者を追悼するミサがこの日に行われた。敗戦後の混乱した生活のなかにありつつも、市民はこうした催事に集い、悲喜こもごもに、終戦を少しずつ実感していった。

　10月21日に、九州配電長崎支店の銭座変電所が復旧し、長崎の街に再び電灯が灯るようになる。11月10日には、被爆後の火災によって焼失した西坂国民学校の替わりに、東中町西勝寺の庫裏や諏訪神社の境内、あるいは借用した民家において、分散授業が開始された。三菱造船所は、軍需機器を民用に転換して鍋や釜や農機具を作り、また戦艦武蔵を建造した船台を利用して55トンの小型漁船を40隻建造した。この頃の長崎市の人口は約14万人、2年後には19万8千人余りに増加する。

　1945年9月16日付の「長崎日日新聞」は、「雲の為"投下狂"ふ／全滅を免れた長崎／爆弾威力は広島の倍」と報じ、これによって長崎市民は、原爆投下をめぐる事実の一端を知った。しかしこれ以後、長崎のみならず全国的に、原爆に関する記述はGHQの厳しい統制下に置かれた。占領軍に対する批判や憎悪に繋がる要素として、また高度な軍事機密に関する要素として、GHQ検閲による規制の対象となったのである。

　報道だけでなく、出版も検閲の対象となった。15歳の女子高生石田雅子の被爆体験記『雅子斃れず』は、自費出版を含めて三度刊行されたが、東京の表現社から刊行される際には、父・石田壽が撮影した被爆写真の収録が大幅に制限された。また永井隆は長崎医科大学助教授として被爆者の治療に従事した報告書をもとに『長崎の鐘』を執筆したが、しかしそのままでの出版は許されず、GHQ諜報課が提供した日本軍によるマニラ市民虐殺の記録「マニラの悲劇」との合本という条件で、出版を許可された。このような検閲は、1949年10月まで続いた。

　さらに長崎軍政部は、原爆に関する機密保持を厳格にする必要から、市民に原爆の関連資料を自発的に提出することを求めた。敗戦から独立までの間、行政を含むあらゆる文書は占領軍の統制下にあり、日本国民の多くは、被爆の実相を実感的に知る術を持たなかったのである。被爆後7年が経ち、講和条約が発効した1952年になると、幾つもの新聞や雑誌が写真入りで原爆特集を組み、それらは驚きをもって読まれた。

被爆都市長崎から観光文化都市長崎へ

　日本の被占領期も後半を迎える頃、今日の長崎を方向付ける2つの大きな動きがあった。

　1つは、1949年8月、「長崎国際文化都市建設法」が公布されたことである。この法律は、「国際文化の向上」と「恒久平和の理想達成」のために、被爆地長崎を「国際文化都市」として建設することを定めた。全国119の戦災都市の復興事業は、その経費の2分の1を国庫補助とするものであったが、この法律により、長崎市の国庫補助は3分の2となったのである。この「国際」「文化」「平和」が一体となった理念は、平和公園や文化

parishioners of Urakami Cathedral perished instantly. Moreover, the vast majority of the approximately 140,000 people killed or injured in the Nagasaki atomic bombing were non-combatant civilians, that is, women, children, teenagers and elderly people. It is estimated that as few as 1,000 soldiers and other men engaged in military service were among the victims.

A crescent moon appeared in the night sky. The following morning the sun rose on a sultry summer day, shedding light on the countless dead and dying victims and blackened corpses strewn throughout the ruins of the city. Parks, schoolyards, and town plazas became makeshift crematoria.

On August 15, 1945 (local time), Japan agreed to the conditions of the Potsdam Declaration and accepted defeat in World War II. People around the world rejoiced at the news.

Thrown into the deepest pit of destitution and misery, the people began their new lives like hungry ghosts, erecting slipshod shelters to fend off the rain, coaxing vegetables from the ravaged soil of the atomic wasteland, and pouring every last bit of strength into the endless bitter struggle to stay alive … Now we can look back quietly on the past, but, despite the elimination of front lines and home fronts under the idyllic placard of 'world peace,' we see the path of hardships and sorrow that we have traversed to date and realize the immensity of the sacrifice foisted upon us as a result of cooperation in war.
(Fukahori Tatsuo, "Shiren" [Ordeal] in *Areno*, Vol. 2, published in November 1947 by the Urakami Catholic Youth Organization)

The people of Urakami lost their possessions, families and friends and picked up the pieces of their lives amid the pungent stench of death. But they persevered, building shacks from scorched sheets of corrugated metal and eking out a meager existence in the aftermath of the atomic bombing.

The twin belfries of old are gone
The church, standing in the dying light,
Is ravaged and noble
(Yoshii Doi, principal of Yamazato Primary School, in *Areno*, Vol. 2)

Urakami Cathedral was reduced to rubble. Urakami Daiichi Hospital, later to become St. Francis Hospital, escaped the conflagration. The missionaries' dining hall on the first floor, a room of 66 square meters in area, was converted into a temporary chapel and its windows covered with straw mats by the surviving faithful of Urakami. On November 23, 1945, a Mass to pray for the souls of the atomic bomb victims was held in the ruins of Urakami Cathedral and provided the first postwar opportunity for the parishioners to gather in one place. Speaking in front of 600 survivors, Fr. Urakawa Wasaburo, a native of Urakami, recited the names of the victims and conducted a memorial sermon. "Urakami has been reduced to a wasteland," he said. "When our forebears returned from the 'journey' in 1873 they found their homes ramshackle but still standing. Today, however, not a single house remains."

The congregation burst into tears at these words. Indeed, nothing was left. And yet there was no other choice but to stand up on this spot and begin again.

All of the atomic bomb survivors, in Urakami and elsewhere, faced day after day of hardships with no resort, sick in body and mind, orphaned and alone, and burdened with the further stigma of social discrimination. Although the exact numbers will never be known, it is said that about one in four of the people who survived direct exposure to the atomic bombing committed suicide. Exposure to the atomic bombing also translated into fear of late effects and death. In the midst of unbearable difficulties and misery, the survivors were unable either to lead a normal existence or even to face death as human beings. This is the reality in which these people found themselves.

Rumors had it that no trees or plants would grow in the atomic wasteland for 70 years because of radio-contamination. Little more than a month after the atomic bombing, however, weeds sprouted from the soil. Encouraged by this rejuvenation of nature, people began to plow the ground in open spaces and sow vegetable seeds.

The small bell hanging in the belfry of Urakami Cathedral had been crushed in the blast, but the large bell was discovered intact in the ruins of the church

会館の建設事業、あるいは幹線道路や土地区画整備などの土木事業という形で実施された。

　もう一つは、1950年10月、日本観光地選定会議・毎日新聞社主催の全国投票「日本観光地百選」都邑の部において、長崎市が95万票を獲得し、京都市や鎌倉市を引き離し、秩父市を5千票の僅差で押さえて第1位となったことである。これは長崎市が、投票に際して、市民の協力を呼びかけた結果であったとされる。戦前期の長崎市は、工業や商業を中心とする港湾都市であったが、諏訪神社散策や雲仙国立公園遊覧などの他に観光施設が整備されておらず、一般的な意味での観光都市という性格を明確に持たなかった。この時期から被爆都市長崎のイメージは、「国際」「文化」「平和」という理念のもとで、観光文化都市という形に集約されていくのである。

　田川務長崎市長は、1953年度の予算編成の方針説明において、観光事業推進を重点施策の一つとし、平和祈念像建設費に400万円、興福寺山門復旧・崇福寺防災工事・高島秋帆邸補修や出島オランダ屋敷復元などに500万を計上する。しかし今日から見れば、こうした観光事業の推進よりも、行政には、戦争による被害を受けた人びと、とりわけ被爆者への対応が求められていた。

　街の復興が進む一方で、被爆者は単に一般的な「戦災者」として分類され、必要な治療を受けることが出来ずにいた。被占領期には、先に述べたようにGHQの検閲によって原爆に関する情報伝達が妨げられていたが、1952年に占領が終わることで、長崎市による原爆障害者の調査や、長崎大学医学部による原爆症患者の無料診療などもはじまり、世論も高まるようになった。1953年1月、長崎市婦人会が被爆者救援のための募金活動を開始する。そして同年8月、衆参の両議院は、広島と長崎の両市長が提出した原爆障害者への治療費援助の請願を採択し、11月にはそのための原爆症調査が始まった。しかし被爆者健康手帳を交付し、医療費の給付等を行う「原子爆弾被爆者の医療等に関する法律」の成立は、1957年3月まで待たなければならなかった。お年玉年賀葉書の寄付金を財源に長崎原爆病院が開設されたのは、1958年5月のことであった。

　被爆者は、心身にハンディを背負い、家族や知友の絆を断たれ、就職や結婚などの機会を不当に狭められ、被爆後の重い人生を背負って生きたのである。瓦礫となった被爆天主堂は、このような困難のなか懸命に生きる人間たちをじっと見守るように、浦上の丘に立っていた。

被爆天主堂の解体

　現在の長崎には、破壊の爪痕を物語る被爆遺構は残存していない。このことから、すでに半世紀以上が経過した今日にあっても、被爆天主堂が失われたことを悔やむ声が折りに触れて聞こえてくる。

　　もし浦上天主堂の残骸があれば、まさにシンボルであった。それに代わるものとして、一九五五年に建立された平和公園内の巨大な「平和祈念像」がある。（中略）しかし、この像に対しては忌避的な見方をする者も多く、全市民的な立場ではシンボルとはなり得ていない」（濱崎均「広島原爆ドームと長崎原爆中心碑の光と影」1997年10月『証言──ヒロシマ・ナガサキの声』）

　　広島の原爆ドームが市民の日常風景の中に溶け込み、怒りの象徴になっているのに比して、廃墟の浦上天主堂を取り壊した長崎には目に見える「語り部」が存在しない。（馬場周一郎「ナガサキの断層・下」（2002年8月9日付「西日本新聞」）

　本書の写真から伝わってくるのは、あの瞬間の極限的な凄まじさを雄弁に語る、被爆遺構の威容である。未曾有の破壊から再生しつつあるこの地で、朗らかに生きようとする人びとを包む、その柔らかなたたずまいである。解体撤去される以前にも、この被爆天主堂の喪失を惜しむ声があったとすれば、それはどのような経過をたどったのだろうか。

　『原爆遺構 長崎の記憶』（1993年、海鳥社）は、被爆天主堂の保存を訴える声が、早い段階からあったことを記している。原爆投下から2ヵ月後の1945年10月6日、長崎市議国友鼎が、市の全員協議会で、被爆遺構の保存について対策をたてるべきことを提議した。

and re-hung in a temporary bell tower built of cedar logs. Rung on Christmas Eve 1945, the toll echoed over the Urakami district for the first time since the atomic bombing. The Catholic faithful trembled with joy at the sound of the "Bell of Nagasaki." A symphony of emotions rose up in each heart, but the sadness was boundless. The temporary wooden bell tower was replaced with an iron-frame structure in December the following year.

An orphan raises hands in prayer
In front of a toppled grave marker
(Moriuchi Hideo, "Fūshi" [Wind Song] in *Areno*, Vol. 2)

The people avoided starvation by eating fried stalks and seeds. A meal of sweet potatoes or pumpkin was a feast. The light of faith, however, never stopped glowing in this austere lifestyle. The population began to grow, replenished by repatriating soldiers and people returning from former colonies overseas. Before long the temporary chapel was too cramped to accommodate the congregation. The people went to the mountains and cut timber and in November 1946 built a new temporary church with a floor space of about 565 square meters beside the ruins of Urakami Cathedral. In March 1948, they also constructed a community center and reserved part of the second story for use as a rectory.

Japan was now under the jurisdiction of foreign military forces. Never before in its long history had it ever experienced such a fate. The General Headquarters of the Supreme Commander for the Allied Powers (GHQ-SCAP) exercised complete authority over Japan and established regional military government teams in 46 prefectures, with the exception of Okinawa. The primary duty of the Nagasaki Military Government Team, which began operation in the former Nagasaki Customs building, was the disarmament and surveillance of the Japanese public. This foreign jurisdiction continued until January 1950.

On October 8, 1945—almost two months after the atomic bombing—the Japanese-language newspaper *Nagasaki Shimbun* carried reports on two events in Nagasaki. One was the beginning the three-day Nagasaki Kunchi Festival; the other was a Mass held in the atomic wasteland and attended by "1,000 faithful living in cave shelters."

The former article described the various performances presented by the people of downtown Nagasaki at the autumn festival, which had been curtailed during the war. Although only part of the usual presentations, the festival was thus revived immediately after Japan's surrender and the end of the conflict.

On the other hand, the latter article reported on the primitive conditions persisting in the hypocenter area of Urakami and a memorial Mass held prior to the general Mass on November 23 mentioned previously. One event is tinted with joy and the other with grief, but they reveal that the people of Nagasaki were finally able to gather for events such as these and to feel the relief of freedom from war.

On October 21, 1945, the Kyushu Electric Company restored its transformer in Zenza-machi, and electric lights came on in Nagasaki for the first time in more than two months. On November 10, Nishizaka Primary School, which had burned to the ground as a result of the atomic bombing, resumed classes in a number of locations around the city including a warehouse at Saishoji Temple in Higashi-nakamachi, an empty outdoor space at Suwa Shinto Shrine, and rooms borrowed in private residences. At the Mitsubishi Nagasaki Shipyard, the equipment used previously to produce munitions was converted for the manufacture of pots, caldrons and farm tools, and several dozen 55-ton fishing boats were constructed on the building berth where the battleship *Musashi* had taken shape the previous decade. Now about 140,000, the population of Nagasaki would climb to more than 198,000 in a matter of only two years.

In its September 16, 1945 issue, the *Nagasaki Nichi Nichi Shimbun* carried an article informing the public for the first time that the Nagasaki atomic bomb had been dropped off-target and that the center of the city had been spared the brunt of destruction, even though the bomb had been almost twice as powerful as that dropped on Hiroshima. From this time onward, however, articles about the atomic bombings were strictly censored throughout Japan by GHQ-SCAP, a measure taken by the Americans to defuse criticism and hatred

こはれ果てたあの工場の跡、焼けのこつた樹木、崩れおちた浦上の天主堂等あらゆるものが大事な研究の資料等だ、人類の責務において我等はこの被害のあとを詳細に記録せねばならぬのだ。(「長崎新聞」1945年10月8日付)

その後の1949年4月、原爆資料保存委員会が、長崎市長の諮問機関として発足した。原爆関連資料の収集や整理が目的であった。同委員会は、天主堂が解体される1958年まで、27回の会合を持ち、9度に渡る浦上天主堂の保存決議を行い、これを市長に伝えたとされる。

1951年9月1日付「長崎日日新聞」の文化欄は、「浦上天主堂存廃是か非か」との特集を組み、これを真正面から取り上げた。記事には、先に触れた『雅子斃れず』の著者石田雅子の父・石田壽が次のようなコメントを寄せている。

立派な芸術品として原爆の記念として観光的にもまた平和運動的にもぜひ長崎市として残すべきものと信じます。あれを壊わしたら一体長崎は原爆の跡として何を残す心算でしよう、原爆の跡なんか無くして一切新にするのだというのなら国際文化都市なんという大それた特別都市になつたことの原因根拠を自ら忘却している

長崎地方裁判所長から京都地方裁判所長に転任した石田壽は、原爆資料保存委員会の前委員長でもあった。石田は、長崎市がこれまで大した援助もせずに放っておいたこと、そのような経緯のなかで世界的観光地として保存すべきと言っても、信者や教会が有り難がるわけもないことを述べ、計上された「保存費百万円」がすぐに削られてしまったことを批判している。しかし、ザビエル400年祭という世界的祭典の場所であったことだけでも被爆天主堂は残す価値があり、「長崎のために! いやや世界人類の平和のために!」保存を希望する、と主張している。また、長崎市議会事務局長の木野普見雄は、新しい世代への平和教育の教材としてとりあげている学校もあること、外国の観光客が皆保存を希望していることを述べている。

他方、信徒の一人は、この間の動きについて、「敷地の都合上新築するなら取りこわすより仕様がないではないか、いつか当局の方が保存費を調査にきて百数十万円を要するといつたきり音沙汰なしです」と語りながらも、「子孫にみせたい」とも付け加え、信徒としての複雑な心境をのぞかせている。カトリック長崎教区長山口愛次郎司教は、ヨーロッパでは同様の情況において、新建築物に遺構を嵌め込む工法が行われていることを紹介する。ただし、「別な面からみれば」とした上で、

アメリカ人が原爆被災地を訪れ、決して誇らかなものとは思わぬだろう、つまりイヤな記念物として映じるものと思われる

と、悲惨な印象を与える遺構であることを憂慮している。この記事はまた、「この問題は長崎県市民の大多数に関心がうすい」こと、しかしこの被爆遺構をどうするかということが「講和ということを前にして、微妙な省察を必要とする」ことを記している。

仮聖堂は手狭となり、生きた魂を救うためにも、本聖堂の再建は必要であった。しかも、近世の長い苦難に耐え、キリシタン復活がなされた信仰の地に建てられた浦上天主堂の存在は大きく、本聖堂の再建は、一地域の一教会再建にとどまらない重要な意味を持っていた。天主堂の再建を望む人たちは、おそらくこの時期、長崎市政の動きをじっと見詰めていたに違いない。

こうしたなかで、やがて浦上教会は、新しい聖堂の建築を本格的に検討し始める。1954年7月に、浦上天主堂再建委員会が発足した。浦上天主堂主任司祭中島万利を会長に、小教区顧問森田喜二郎を事務局長とした再建委員会は、全国に「浦上天主堂再建趣意書」を発送して献金を求める。しかし、信徒の積立金や寄付などによる拠出金を合算しても、3千万円が限度であると見積もられ、資金不足が予想された。そのため1955年5月に、山口愛次郎司教が渡米し、米国内の教会施設などを訪問して募金活動を行った。翌年2月に帰国した山口は、信愛幼稚園講堂において、廃墟である被爆天主堂を解体撤

over the use of the atomic bombs and to protect military secrets.

Books as well as newspaper reportage were subjected to censorship. Fifteen year-old high school student Ishida Masako published three editions of *Masako Taorezu* (Masako Carries On), a memoir of her experience of the Nagasaki atomic bombing. When it was published by Hyogensha of Tokyo, however, the photographs of Nagasaki taken by the author's father Hisashi were drastically reduced in number. Similarly, Nagai Takashi penned a book entitled *Nagasaki no Kane* (The Bell of Nagasaki) recounting his work in assisting the atomic bomb victims as an assistant professor at Nagasaki Medical College, but the GHQ-SCAP Intelligence Section banned the book as it stood and agreed to its publication only after the addition of a chapter entitled "The Tragedy of Manila" documenting the slaughter of civilians by Japanese forces in the Philippines. This censorship continued until October 1949.

Moreover, the Nagasaki Military Government Team called upon the citizens of this city to voluntarily turn over all atomic bomb-related materials and artifacts, citing the necessity to protect military secrets. From the time of defeat until the departure of the Occupation forces, all public and private documents were subject to restrictions imposed by the Occupation government, leaving the majority of Japanese people completely in the dark about the atomic bombings and their aftermath. Only after the San Francisco Peace Treaty of 1952 did Japanese newspapers begin to publish articles and photographs dealing with the atomic bombings. Needless to say, these were viewed with astonishment by the Japanese public.

From Atomic Wasteland to City of Tourism and Culture

Two major events in the latter part of the Occupation Period set a new direction for the city of Nagasaki. One was the promulgation of the "Nagasaki International Culture City Construction Law" in August 1949. This law called for the re-construction of Nagasaki as an international culture city in order to "elevate international culture" and to "achieve the ideal of lasting world peace." In another 119 devastated cities around Japan, half of the money needed to implement re-construction projects was provided through national relief funds, but in Nagasaki's case the national government provided two-thirds of the necessary financing. Launched on the basis of a concept amalgamating "international," "culture" and "peace," the work here included the construction of Peace Park and the Nagasaki Culture Hall as well as civil engineering works such as the refurbishment of main roads and re-zoning of neighborhoods.

The second epoch-making event was Nagasaki's victory in the "Best Hundred Tourist Destinations in Japan Contest" held jointly by a selection committee and the newspaper *Mainichi Shimbun* in October 1950. Nagasaki took first place in the city category, surpassing Kyoto and Kamakura with 950,000 votes and winning over the runner-up Chichibu by a margin of 5,000 votes. This result is said to have been affected by Nagasaki City's appeal to local citizens for cooperation. Nagasaki had flourished during the prewar years as a port city centering on industrial and commercial enterprises, but, aside from walks in Suwa Shinto Shrine and tours of Unzen National Park, there were few well-equipped tourist facilities in the area and no clear "tourist city" character in the usual sense of the term. Now the image of Nagasaki changed from that of a city recovering from the devastation of the atomic bombing to one of a city of tourism and culture reinventing itself under the concepts of "international," "culture" and "peace."

In his announcement of budget policy for the year 1953, Mayor Tagawa Tsutomu cited the promotion of tourism as a high priority, allocating four million yen for the construction of a peace-related monument and five million yen for other projects such as the restoration of the main gate at Kofukuji Temple, disaster prevention work at Sofukuji Temple, repairs to the former Takashima Shuhan residence, and the restoration of the former Dutch Factory at Dejima. In retrospect, however, government assistance to the victims of war and especially the atomic bomb survivors was of vastly more importance than the promotion of tourism.

While the reconstruction of the city progressed, the atomic bomb survivors were placed in the same category with other war damage sufferers and received no special medical attention. Information on the

旧浦上天主堂、西側からの空撮。1953年。画面右半分中央やや上、円形の敷地に見えるのが天主堂廃墟。右に仮聖堂、手前の道沿いに公民館が見える。右側に道をはさんで長崎大学医学部グラウンド。

Urakami Cathedral seen from the sky to the west in 1953. The circular plot of land in the right upper central part of the photograph is the ruins of the cathedral. The temporary church and community center are visible on the right. The large open lot across the road to the right is the sports field at Nagasaki University Faculty of Medicine.

去し、同じ場所に新天主堂を再建する構想を信徒に説明した。また、当初保存に前向きだった田川務市長が、ある時期から解体撤去へと傾き、このことについて市民の間では、様々な噂や憶測も囁かれた。こうして天主堂の再建計画が、保存のための議論に先行して進んでいったのである。

1958年1月、長崎市国際文化会館会議室で開かれた原爆資料保存委員会の席上においてのことである。委員の1人でもある中島万利司祭が、浦上教会として、2月から廃墟の解体撤去の工事を開始する予定であると告げた。被爆から13年が経ち、浦上一帯は道路が拡張され、家々が建ち、観光客も増えた。この間、原爆の痕跡は次々に消し去られ、そして大きな被爆遺構としては、被爆天主堂が唯一のものとなっていた。

このようななかで、2月17日、第2回長崎臨時市議会が開催された。岩口夏夫議員は、「浦上天主堂の遺跡保存問題に対する市長の見解」と題する質問を行い、市長の所信を問いただし、保存に最大限努力することを要望する。これに対して田川務市長は、代替地取得などによって、被爆天主堂を保存するつもりはないと答弁した。

atomic bombings had been blocked by GHQ-SCAP censorship, but, when the Occupation Period ended in 1952, public awareness increased in conjunction with Nagasaki City's surveys on the late effects of atomic bomb exposure and free medical treatment for atomic bomb survivors conducted by Nagasaki University Medical School. In January 1953, the Nagasaki Women's Association launched a fundraising campaign for the atomic bomb survivors. In August the same year, the upper and lower houses of the Japanese National Diet adopted a petition submitted by the mayors of Hiroshima and Nagasaki for medical assistance to the sufferers in the two cities, and a preliminary medical survey was started in November. However, only in March 1957 would the "Law Regarding the Medical Treatment of Atomic Bomb Sufferers" provide for the issuing of survivor health cards and financial relief from medical costs. In May 1958, the Nagasaki Atomic Bomb Hospital was opened with the help of funding from a New Year's greeting card lottery.

The atomic bomb survivors were burdened with physical and mental handicaps, separated from family and friends, and unfairly disadvantaged in employment and marriage opportunities. During the years of pain and hardship after the war, the ruins of Urakami Cathedral stood on the hillside looking down on these dire circumstances and silently encouraging the people in their efforts to build a new life.

The Removal of the Ruins of Urakami Cathedral

Few if any scars of the atomic bombing are visible in modern-day Nagasaki. If only for this reason, even though more than half a century has passed, cries of regret over the loss of the old Urakami Cathedral can still be heard today.

建築中の新天主堂。南西上空から。1959年。

The new Urakami Cathedral (under construction) seen from the sky to the southwest in 1959.

If the ruins of Urakami Cathedral remained they would be a powerful symbol. Instead we have the huge 'Peace Statue' erected in Peace Park in 1955… However, many people tend to shun this statue, and it has failed to become a symbol generally embraced by the citizens of Nagasaki.
(Hamasaki Hitoshi, "Hiroshima Genbaku Dōmu to Nagasaki Genbaku Chūshinhi no Hikari to Kage" [Light and Dark of the Hiroshima Atomic Bomb Dome and Nagasaki Hypocenter Monument] in *Shōgen—Hiroshima to Nagasaki no Koe*, October 1997)

The Hiroshima Atomic Bomb Dome has blended into the daily scenery of life in the city and become an

さらに市長がこの被爆天主堂をどのように考えているのか、翌日の「長崎日日新聞」は次のように伝えている。

> あの残がいが観光資源になつていることはまちがいないが"平和"のために役立つているとは思わない。原爆の恐ろしさはすでに科学的に証明されているので、この廃墟があろうがなかろうが問題ではないと思う。教会側の都合で取りこわされても仕方ない保存策（ママ）については最初から熱意も政治力もなく、また財源もなかつた

それでも翌日の市議会は、議員提出「旧浦上天主堂の原爆資料保存に関する決議案」を全会一致で可決し、保存対策への善処を求めた。これを受けて、市長は山口愛次郎司教と会見し、また議会も天主堂保存の要請を行ったが、結局は不調に終わり、撤去の方針を翻すことは出来なかった。

1958年3月14日、ついに浦上天主堂の解体撤去作業が始まる。「被爆の証人」は、ハンマーで打ち砕かれ、万力で引き倒された。市内最大の被爆遺構は跡形もなくなり、ただ南側壁の一部だけが、市議会の最後の決定によって、爆心地公園に移築保存されることになった。

過去への回路

> 広島の取り組みをみるとき、廃墟保存を全市的運動にまで押し広げることができなかった長崎の思想的未成熟を思わざるを得ない。天主堂喪失——それは核時代の歴史力に欠けた長崎市民自身の敗北であった（馬場周一郎「ナガサキの断層」中、2002年8月8日付「西日本新聞」）

広島の原爆ドームが世界遺産としての価値を認められている今日、この記事が指摘する通り、被爆天主堂の喪失は、ある種の「敗北」として考えられるべきなのかもしれない。

しかし、広島の原爆ドームの保存を訴える最初の行動は、1960年5月のことである。白血病によって12歳で亡くなった被爆者佐々木禎子を悼み、1958年に結成された「広島折鶴の会」の子どもたちと、その世話人である私立大学校務員の河本一郎が、原爆ドームの保存に向けた署名と募金を呼び掛けたことから、この被爆遺構の保存運動が始まった。それまでは、「自分のアバタ面を世界に誇示し同情を引こうとする貧乏人根性を、広島市民はもはや精算しなければいけない」(1948年10月10日付「夕刊ひろしま」)と解体撤去を主張する記事もあったほどであり、こうした保存の呼び掛けに対しても、しばらくの間は目立った反応もなく、むしろ知事や市長、地元紙の論調は、これを解体して美しい平和都市ヒロシマを復興することに傾いていた。保存への熱意が、市民の賛意を得られるようになりはじめたのは、1964年のことであった。原爆ドームは、こうした経緯のなかで、2度の保存工事を経て、ヒロシマを象徴する被爆遺構となり、1996年12月にユネスコ世界遺産に登録されたのである。

広島の保存運動が、60年代の始めであったことに対し、長崎で天主堂の存廃が問題になったのは50年代であった。この時期の長崎は、復興に追われ、また被爆後の現実とたたかい、生きることに懸命でなければならなかった。余力がなく、市民の力も十分に培われていない時期であった。また、県の産業奨励館であった原爆ドームに比べ、浦上天主堂は信仰の拠り所として、生きた魂を救い続けなければならない役割を負っていた。浦上信徒の願いは、どこかに本聖堂を再建しなければならないということで一貫していた。再建される場所が、長い苦難の歴史をもつその地でなければならないという思いに対し、さらになお保存運動を主張し続けることが容易であったとは思われない。こうした点を踏まえると、「敗北」という言葉は酷なのではないだろうか。

当初は被爆天主堂の保存に前向きだった田川市長が、いつしか解体撤去へ姿勢を転換させた背後に、市長が1955年12月に渡米した経緯との関わりを見いだし、そこに何らかの隠された意図や懐柔策があったのではないかという推論もある。市長の1ヵ月に渡る米国滞在は、米国ミネソタ州セントポール市と長崎市が、日本初の姉妹都市提携を決議したことに伴い、セントポール市からの招きに応じたものだった。高瀬毅『ナガサキ 消えたもう一つの「原爆ドーム」』(2009年、平凡社)はこの問題

emotional symbol. By contrast, the ruins of Urakami Cathedral were removed from Nagasaki and nothing is left to physically relate the truth of the atomic bombing.
(Baba Shuichiro, "Nagasaki no Dansō-3" [Nagasaki Crevice, Part 3] in *Nishinihon Shimbun*, August 9, 2002)

What emerges from the photographs in the present book is the majesty of an atomic bomb ruin speaking silently but eloquently of the ferocity of that earth-shattering instant, a gentle presence enveloping a generation of people trying to rebuild their lives from the ashes of an unprecedented calamity. Assuming that they were heard, what happened to the cries of regret emitted before the removal of the ruins?

The book *Genbaku Ikō—Nagasaki no Kioku* [Atomic Bomb Ruins—The Memory of Nagasaki] (Kaichosha, 1993) recounts the fact that calls for the preservation of the ruins of Urakami Cathedral were heard from an early stage. Speaking at a plenary session of the Nagasaki City Council on October 6, 1945, less than two months after the atomic bombing, Councilman Kunitomo Kanae submitted a proposal stating that measures should be taken to preserve the atomic bomb ruins:

The broken remains of factories, the scorched stumps of trees, the crumbling carcass of Urakami Cathedral—all of these are important subjects for research. It is our responsibility to humanity to carefully record the details of this destruction.
(*Nagasaki Nichi Nichi Shimbun*, October 8, 1945)

Some four years later in April 1949, the Atomic Bomb Artifacts Preservation Committee gathered as an advisory body under the mayor of Nagasaki. The purpose was to collect and organize artifacts and materials related to the atomic bombing. Records show that committee meetings were convened 27 times prior to the removal of the ruins of Urakami Cathedral in 1958 and that on nine occasions the committee adopted a resolution calling for the preservation of the ruins and submitted this to the mayor.

In the culture column in its September 1, 1951 issue, the *Nagasaki Nichi Nichi Shimbun* carried a special article under the title "Should Urakami Cathedral Be Preserved?" Ishida Hisashi, the father of Ishida Masako mentioned earlier as the author of the atomic bomb memoir *Masako Taorezu* (Masako Carries On), is quoted as follows:

I believe that Nagasaki City, from the perspective of both tourism and the peace movement, should preserve the cathedral as a wonderful work of art and as a testimony to the atomic bombing. If it is demolished, what does Nagasaki intend to preserve as a reminder of the atomic bombing? If a decision is made to remake everything anew without preserving the atomic bomb ruins, then it will prove that Nagasaki has deliberately forgotten the reason for its special designation as an 'international culture city.'

Ishida Hisashi had served as chairman of the Atomic Bomb Artifacts Preservation Committee before his appointment as president of the Kyoto District Court. He leveled criticism at Nagasaki for neglecting the ruins of Urakami Cathedral and for slashing the one million yen budget allotted for preservation—even though city leaders had recognized the value of the ruins as a world-class tourism resource—on the grounds that the parishioners and church elders would not welcome the preservation project. Ishida insisted that the role of the cathedral as the site of the international commemoration of the 400th anniversary of St. Francis Xavier's arrival in Japan was sufficient to justify its preservation, and he expressed a hope to safeguard the ruins "for the sake of Nagasaki, no, for the sake of all humankind!" Kino Fumio, chief of the Nagasaki City Council Secretariat, supported this opinion, pointing out that several schools were using the ruins as a teaching material for the peace education of a new generation and that foreign visitors to Nagasaki unanimously advocated preservation.

On the other hand, one parishioner said, "The conditions of the property are such that the removal of the ruins seems inevitable. An official from city hall came to the site and estimated that more than a million yen was needed for preservation, but we never heard from him again." He added nevertheless that, "I want my

改装後の浦上天主堂。2008年。Urakami Cathedral after refurbishments in 2008.

について、在米資料を傍証とし、あるいは当事者の証言などを拾いながら、冷戦下における米国の民間外交施策との関連を解明しようと試みている。

　こうした事柄に、より客観的な論証を加えるためには、さらなる証言や記録を必要とする。しかし、未だに生々しい現代史の領域に属することである。はっきりとしない周辺事情、あるいは当事者の胸にそのままに仕舞われた思いがあるのかもしれない。また在米資料を含め、重要な記録が未発掘なのかもしれないが、とりわけ、1958年3月、長崎市役所の火災があって、関連資料が失われてしまったことなどが、さまざまな追確認の作業を困難にしている。

　こうした被爆天主堂解体の裏面にあったかもしれない事情を証し立てることとは別の回路から、私たちが過去の出来事に向かい合うことは、果たして不可能であろうか？

　1963年に発表された井上光晴の『地の群れ』は、1950年代の浦上に「海塔新田」という架空の「部落」を設定し、敗戦後のこの地に生きる人びとの姿と情念を、虚実を織り交ぜて描いた小説である。作品中、津山信夫が前を行く修道女の背を見ながら、瓦礫と化した浦上天主堂にまつわる、ある記憶をたどる。それは4年前の5月、雨が降りしきる浦上天主堂の廃墟で、顔半分を熱線で黒く灼かれたマリア像を見ていた時のことであった。そのマリア像を自分のものにしたいという考えが、ふと津山にひらめく。

　　浦上天主堂の撤去問題が長崎市議会で取り上げら

children and grandchildren to see the ruins," revealing the complicated emotions of the Catholic faithful in Urakami. Fr. Yamaguchi Aijiro, Catholic Bishop of Nagasaki, pointed out that, in European churches damaged in wartime, restoration methods were adopted to incorporate the ruins into newly constructed buildings. He is also quoted as saying that, "From another viewpoint, American visitors to the areas afflicted by the atomic bombing are unlikely to feel any pride. Indeed, in their eyes, the ruins are only an unpleasant reminder."

The newspaper article concludes that "the great majority of citizens of Nagasaki prefecture and city have little interest in the issue" but that the decision regarding the fate of the ruins of Urakami Cathedral "requires, in the face of the impending peace treaty, subtle reflection and consideration."

The temporary church was cramped and, if only to save the living souls of the people, the reconstruction of the cathedral was imperative. However, the old Urakami Cathedral carried enormous weight as the place of worship built on land where the Catholic faithful had endured centuries of persecution and celebrated the revival of their religion in Japan. Indeed, the significance of the issue went far beyond the simple restoration of a neighborhood church. The people hoping for the reconstruction of the cathedral undoubtedly waited on tenterhooks for the decision of the municipal administration of Nagasaki.

Before long the people of Urakami were considering in earnest the construction of a new cathedral, and the Urakami Cathedral Restoration Committee came together in July 1954 to deal with the issue. Fr. Nakashima Banri, rector of Urakami Cathedral, and Morita Kijiro, diocese consultant, assumed the posts of chairman and secretary-general, respectively. The committee distributed a prospectus on the restoration project and called for donations from around Japan. It became clear, however, that the funds accumulated by the Catholic faithful combined with donations would amount to no more than 30 million yen and thus prove insufficient. In May 1955, Bishop Yamaguchi Aijiro traveled to the United States and visited Catholic facilities around the country to drum up support for the project. When he returned to Nagasaki in February the

現在の浦上天主堂。1997 年、DEITz 提供。

Urakami Cathedral as it looks today.
Taken in 1997, Courtesy of DEITz.

following year, he convened a meeting in the auditorium of Shin'ai Kindergarten and announced a plan to remove the ruins of the old cathedral and erect a new building on the same site. Mayor Tagawa Tsutomu, who had initially favored the preservation of the ruins, also began at some point to support their removal, a change of policy that elicited various rumors and speculation among the citizens of Nagasaki. In this way, the plan to rebuild the cathedral took precedence over the discussion related to preservation.

In January 1958, a meeting of the Atomic Bomb Artifacts Preservation Committee was held in the conference room of the Nagasaki City International Culture Hall. Fr. Nakashima Banri, who was also a committee member, announced that the work to remove the ruins of Urakami Cathedral would begin the following month. Thirteen years had passed since the atomic bombing. Roads had been widened in the Urakami district, houses had been built, and the number of tourists was increasing. As a result, one atomic bomb scar after another had been erased, leaving the ruins of Urakami Cathedral as the last large-scale reminder in the city.

On February 17, an extraordinary meeting of Nagasaki City Council was convened, and Councilman

れた時、「原爆の廃墟は平和のためというより、無残な過去の思い出につながりすぎる。憎悪をかきたてるだけのああいう建物は一日も早く取りこわしたほうがいい」という大浦天主堂の司教に対して、ある被爆女性の語った言葉を新聞記事か何かで読んだことがあるが、マリヤ像がかわりにその苦しみを訴えているように彼は感じた。

三菱電機製作所に学徒動員中原爆にあい、脊髄骨折のため、以来十三年間下半身不随の身を病床に横たえている二十八歳のその女性は、原爆映画『生きていてよかった』のロケで、戦後はじめて母親と一緒にタクシーに乗り、浦上天主堂の焼けただれたマリヤ像を見たのだが、その時の強烈な印象を思いうかべながら訴えたのである。

「あの時、マリヤの顔が半分、放射能で黒くやけているのをみましたが、もしあのマリヤ像が人間ならケロイドになっているでしょう。ケロイドはたしかに醜い、しかし、生きた人間はその残酷な姿をさらしてどこまでも生きていかねばなりません。その人が強く生きようとすればするほど、ケロイドは醜くなります。顔半分焼けたマリヤ様にも、そういうふうに生きてもらいたいのです。むずかしい理屈はわかりませんが、あの天主堂の廃墟が、どうして教会の人がいうように、憎しみを忘れさせないものとなるのか、私は平和ということ以外にあの像を想像することができません」

そのようなことを思い起こしつつ、津山は、いつかどこかに持ち運びだされてしまうかも知れないという切迫した思いから、マリア像の首を盗むのであるが、暗闇の中、それを誤って落としてしまう。唐米袋から転がり出たマリア像の首は、「原子爆弾でやられた人間の生首のように」見え、「浦上で爆死した信者の死体が、首を返せといいながら何人も何人も追ってくるような」思いに駆られて、その像を打ち砕いてしまう。

翌日信者たちは、津山を疑い、責め立てる。一人の信者の男は彼に、先祖代々殉教者の血がしみこんだ地に、長い時をかけてようやく完成した天主堂は、「信者タチノ血ト涙ノ祈リト歴史ガコメラレテイタノダ」と迫る。もう一人の信者の男は、「自分たちの土地に、自分たちの積み立てた力で新しい教会堂を建てるのに、横から一銭の協力もせず、さあ廃墟を残せ、平和のシンボルだと叫んでも筋が通らぬ」と、「その責任まで全部彼にあるかのように」喚く。天主堂を訪れる観光客が、ミサを行う信徒にまで、うるさくカメラのシャッターを切っていたり、動物園でものぞくようなアベックの嬌声があがったりすることの理不尽さも、信者は津山にぶちまけるのであった。

ソンナラバ、ソンナ血ト涙ノ祈リガコメラレテイル尊イ聖地ナラバ、ナゼ原子爆弾ガ落チタノカ。昭和二十年八月九日午前十一時二分、浦上教会区一万二千名ノ信者ノウチ、八千五百名ガ滅ビテシマッタガ、ソンナラバ、キリストノ神様ガ選ンダコノ地ニナゼ原子爆弾ヲ落シタノカ。その時考えたことをいま考えているのか、その時そう考えればよかったと考えているのか、混沌とした頭の中に、ふと彼自身びっくりするような、記憶とも思いつきともつかぬ疑問がとびこんできた。ひょっとすると、死んだ母親も浦上の信者ではなかったのか……

この作品は、小説という表現方法に拠る以外には容易に公の場に浮上し得ないような、被爆後の浦上に生きる苦悩や葛藤を、重層的に描出することを試みている。過去を誠実に考察しようとすれば、人びとの錯綜した事情や、秘匿されたかもしれない苦悩、人びとの間にある分断や蔑視を、自らが知らずにいるかもしれないことに意識的でなければならない。掬おうとしても掬い尽くせない感情のもつれ、あるいは私たちが見極めることが出来ると思う以上の複雑に絡み合う現実があることを、慎重に見つめなければならない。

記述されたことは、より多くの記述されなかった生の上に成り立っている。当時の現実、地べたを這うように生きた思いは、過ぎ去る時間と共に、私たちの生活から遠くよそよそしいものになっていく。そればかりではなく、被爆天主堂の不在という事実そのものが、忘れられ

Iwaguchi Natsuo asked for "the mayor's view on the problem of the preservation of the ruins of Urakami Cathedral," inquiring into the latter's convictions on the subject and calling for his utmost efforts in the cause of preservation. Mayor Tagawa responded by saying that he had no intention to preserve the ruins by finding an alternative site for the new cathedral or by any other means. The mayor's views on the ruins of Urakami Cathedral were outlined as follows in an article carried the next day by the *Nagasaki Nichi Nichi Shimbun*:

> It is undeniable that the ruins are a tourism resource, but I do not think that they are serving the purpose of 'peace.' The horror of the atomic bomb has already been documented scientifically, so it does not matter whether or not the ruins exist. If the ruins are removed according to the circumstances of the church, then so be it; from the outset there has been no enthusiasm, no political control, and no available funding for preservation on site.

Nevertheless, Nagasaki City Council voted unanimously the following day to adopt the "resolution regarding the preservation of the atomic bombed ruins of the former Urakami Cathedral" and demanded the adoption of appropriate measures. In response, Mayor Tagawa held a meeting with Bishop Yamaguchi Aijiro, and the city council submitted an official request for preservation, but in the end these efforts failed to overturn the decision to demolish the ruins.

On March 14, 1958, the demolition and removal of the ruins of the former Urakami Cathedral began. The "Witness to the Atomic Bombing" and largest relic in Nagasaki crumbled under the impact of hammers and the pull of vise cables. The only remnant was a portion of the southern wall, moved to Hypocenter Park in accordance with the final decision of Nagasaki City Council.

A Circuit to the Past

> Looking at Hiroshima, one cannot help but be impressed with the ideological immaturity of Nagasaki, which was unable to expand the effort to preserve the ruins into a comprehensive civilian movement. The loss of Urakami Cathedral signified the defeat of the citizens of Nagasaki, their inability to make history in the nuclear age.
> (Baba Shuichiro, "Nagasaki no Dansō-2" [Nagasaki Crevice, Part 2] in *Nishinihon Shimbun*, August 8, 2002)

Today, when the value of the Hiroshima Atomic Bomb Dome has been recognized by designation as a World Heritage, it may indeed be correct to interpret the loss of the former Urakami Cathedral as a kind of "defeat."

However, the movement to preserve the ruins of the Hiroshima Prefectural Industrial Promotion Hall—the "atomic bomb dome"—did not begin until May 1960. A children's group called the "Hiroshima Paper Crane Society" was formed in 1958 to honor atomic bomb victim Sasaki Sadako, who had died of atomic bomb illness at the age of 12. The children and their mentor Kawamoto Ichiro, an employee at a local private university, launched a campaign to preserve the ruined building by collecting signatures and donations. Until then, newspapers had often advocated demolition, the *Yukan Hiroshima*, for example, writing, "It is about time that the people of Hiroshima desist from their despicable habit of displaying a pockmarked face to the world in the hope of attracting sympathy." (October 10, 1948). Even the above preservation campaign failed to elicit any conspicuous response at first. The opinions of the Hiroshima governor and mayor and the tone of newspaper editorials fell in favor of demolishing the ruins and constructing a beautiful new city of peace. Only in 1964 did the aspiration for the preservation of the ruins begin to garner general approval. The Hiroshima Atomic Bomb Dome underwent conservation work on two occasions before becoming an established worldwide symbol of the atomic bombing and finally being added to the UNESCO World Heritage List in December 1996.

While the preservation movement in Hiroshima began in the 1960's, the debate about whether or not to preserve the ruins of Urakami Cathedral occurred during the previous decade, a time when Nagasaki was driven by the imperatives of postwar restoration and the grim reality of the atomic wasteland. No surplus

木彫寄せ木造りの被爆マリア像。1930年にイタリアから輸入され、旧天主堂の正面祭壇最上階に安置されていた。被爆後の瓦礫から、2メートルの像のうち頭部が奇跡的に発見。その後持ち去られて所在不明であったが、ふたたび浦上天主堂に戻され、被爆60周年の2005年8月9日、被爆者のための祈りの場である被爆マリア小聖堂祭壇中央に置かれた。DEITz提供。

A two-meter tall statue of Mary made of wood parquetry was imported from Italy in 1930 and enshrined on the highest level of the main altar in the old Urakami Cathedral. After the atomic bombing, workers found that the head of the statue had remained miraculously intact in the rubble. For a time its whereabouts were unknown, but it was eventually returned to Urakami Cathedral. On the 60th anniversary of the Nagasaki atomic bombing on August 9, 2005, it was enshrined above the altar in a sanctuary created for the prayers of the atomic bomb survivors. (Courtesy of DEITz)

ようとしている。そうした現在、この地にあった様々な思いや立場を想像し、それをたどり直し、近づこうとする時の入り口は、例えば『地の群れ』のような文学作品にも開かれている。記録に残る事柄のみに還元することは出来ない過去の現実を、多様な生の絡み合いとしてたどり直そうとするならば、私たちはこうした文学作品の虚構性を補助線のようにして、事実に並置してみることも必要なのではないか。

浦上天主堂の再建は、被爆天主堂の解体撤去に引き続いて、1958年3月に着工し、1959年10月に完成した。1982年、長崎小教区の信徒戸数は1590戸、信徒数は8944名となり、日本最大の規模となる。1980年に長崎教区は、ローマ教皇に長崎訪問を要請し、ヨハネ・パウロⅡ世の来訪が実現した。これを機に、再建浦上天主堂は銅板張り屋根と赤煉瓦張り外装に改装される。これが、現在私たちが浦上の丘に仰ぎ見る浦上天主堂である。

本書の表紙とした写真には、無邪気に遊ぶ子どもたちが写っている。その多くは、おそらく被爆後の浦上に生まれ、そして被爆後の浦上に育った子どもたちであろう。まさに生命そのものが輝いているような子どもたちを、崩れた壁や傷付いた石像たちが、その背後にあって無言の笑顔で包んでいるかのようである。その廃墟や石像の影に隠れるように、江戸期の浦上、近代の浦上、そして65年前に天主堂とともに崩れ落ちた人びとがひっそりと佇んでいて、喜びのざわめきを添えているようにも感じる。

13年の間、被爆天主堂は、原爆によって深く傷付いた姿のままで浦上の丘に立ち、人びとの生活を見守り続けた。石像たちも、焼け焦げた痛ましい表情によって、被爆の現実を無言のうちに語り続けた。当時の浦上の人びとは、この地にかつて連綿と生き続けてきた人びとを思い、天主堂を創建した人びとを思い、それらを廃墟に重ねて仰ぎ見ていたのであろう。その励ましは、重く、尊いものであった。

被爆した天主堂は、形としては残らなかった。しかし本書の写真が記録した被爆天主堂の姿に、復活と再生の

resources were available, nor had the citizens of Nagasaki developed organizational skills. Moreover, unlike the defunct Hiroshima Prefectural Industrial Promotion Hall, Urakami Cathedral was a place of worship with a responsibility to continue providing religious services to the living. The unanimous wish of the Catholic faithful of Urakami was simply to rebuild their cathedral. For most of them the site of reconstruction could only be the hill at Urakami, steeped as it was in the long history of persecution and endurance, a conviction that ran counter to, and frustrated, the continuing hope to preserve the precious ruins of their church. It seems rather severe, in view of these facts, to condemn their decision with the word "defeat."

As mentioned earlier, Mayor Tagawa Tsutomu initially advocated the preservation of the ruins of Urakami Cathedral but, at some point, shifted in favor of demolition and removal. Some observers, noting that the mayor visited the United States in December 1955, surmise the existence of some hidden motive or conciliatory measure behind the change of stance. The month-long visit was conducted in response to an invitation from the city of Saint Paul, Minnesota in connection with the linking of Nagasaki and Saint Paul in Japan's first sister-city affiliation. In his book *Nagasaki—Kieta mō Hitotsu no Genbaku Dōmu* (Nagasaki—The Loss of the Other 'Atomic Bomb Dome,' Heibonsha, 2009), Takase Takeshi cites corroborating evidence from the United States and testimonials from some of the people involved, attempting to explain Mayor Tagawa's about-face in terms of American civilian diplomatic policy in the Cold War.

Further testimony and documentary evidence are necessary to prove this conjecture objectively. Moreover, the affair still lies in the sensitive realm of recent history. The circumstances are unclear, and certain facts may remain undisclosed in the hearts of the people involved. It is also possible that researchers are yet to unearth important records in the United States or elsewhere. In any case, events such as the destruction of Nagasaki City Hall by fire in March 1958 and loss of invaluable documents greatly impede the process of verification.

Will it ever be possible for us to find another way to shed light on the circumstances of the past, an alternative to trying to prove the existence of a hidden agenda in the demolition of the ruins of Urakami Cathedral?

In his 1963 novel *Chi no Mure* (Apart from Life), Inoue Mitsuharu supposes an imaginary village called "Kaito Shinden" in 1950's Urakami and weaves fiction with historical facts in portraying the people living there in the aftermath of war. In one scene, the protagonist Tsuyama Nobuo notices a nun walking in front of him and recalls experiences related to the ruins of Urakami Cathedral. Four years earlier, standing in the rain at the ruins and looking at a statue of Mary with half its face scorched black by the atomic bombing, he had suddenly felt a desire to keep the statue for himself.

When the fate of the ruins of Urakami Cathedral was under discussion by Nagasaki City Council, a priest from the cathedral was quoted as saying, 'The atomic bomb ruins, far from serving the cause of peace, overly emphasize horrible memories of the past. Buildings that only stir up feelings of hatred should be removed as soon as possible.' Tsuyama remembered reading, in a newspaper article or somewhere else, the words of an atomic bomb survivor in response to this comment, and he felt that the statue of Mary was crying out in pain on her behalf.

The 28 year-old woman quoted in the article had been exposed to the atomic bombing while serving as a mobilized student at the Mitsubishi Electric Works. Suffering from a spinal injury, she had been paralyzed from the waist down and confined to bed for the subsequent 13 years. During the production of the movie *Ikiteite yokatta* (Glad to be Alive), she had taken a taxi with her mother for the first time and seen the statue of Mary at Urakami Cathedral, and she related her intense reaction to it as follows:

'Half of Mary's face was burnt black by exposure to the atomic bombing. If she were human she would have suffered terrible keloid scars. Keloid scars are ugly. How long can a living person go on displaying that hideous form? In fact the stronger a person is, the uglier the keloid scars become. I hope Mary, with half her face scorched black, will live on boldly like that. I cannot understand any difficult the-

歴史がこの地を築いてきたことを重ね合わせてみると、それが今でも、形をかえて生き続けていると感じるのである。

主要参考文献
『信仰の礎』(1930 年、浦上天主堂)
浦川和三郎『浦上キリシタン史』(1943 年、全国書房)
浦上小教区機関紙『荒野(あれの)』(1947 年 8 月 15 日創刊、浦上カトリック連合青年会)
歌川龍平『長崎郷土物語』(1952 年、長崎民友新聞社)
北島宗人編輯『記録写真 原爆の長崎』(1952 年、第一出版社)
山田かん「長崎の原爆記録をめぐって」(『地人』1956 年 11 月)
池松経興『浦上天主堂被爆遺跡写真集』(1959 年、私家版。写真 88 点貼付 100 部限定)
片岡弥吉『浦上天主堂』(1959 年、浦上天主堂)
『カトリック長崎大司教区 100 年のあゆみ』(1965 年、大司教区)
山里浜口地区原爆復元の会編『爆心の丘にて』(1972 年、長崎の証言刊行委員会)
西田秀雄編集『神の家族四〇〇年――浦上小教区沿革史』(1983 年、浦上カトリック教会)
『長崎市議会史――資料編』第 2 巻(1993 年、長崎市議会)
『原爆被爆記録写真集』(1996 年、長崎平和推進協会)
池松経興『落ちた聖像』(1998 年、個人出版)
『浦上天主堂写真集』(1999 年、カトリック浦上教会)

※被占領下の報道規制により、被爆直後の長崎の様子を記録した写真は、数少ない。貴重な例外である山端庸介の写真を参照されたい。

ories, but how do the ruins of the cathedral prevent people from forgetting hatred, as the person from the church says? I for one cannot think of anything but peace when looking at the statue of Mary.'

With these thoughts in his mind, Tsuyama cringes, imagining the possibility that the statue may someday be carried away from the ruins. He steals the head of the statue but accidentally drops it in the darkness. When it rolls out of the sac he was carrying, it reminds him of "the mutilated head of a person decapitated by the atomic bomb." Feeling that hundreds of victims who died in Urakami were chasing him and "demanding the return of the head," he smashes it to pieces.

The following day, the Catholic faithful accuse Tsuyama of the crime. One man cries that the cathedral was built on land soaked with the blood of martyred ancestors and completed after decades of labor and that, "It is steeped in the blood of the faithful and the history of tearful prayer." Says another man: "We want to build a new church on our own land, using the resources we have accumulated ourselves. Without a penny of support, you demand that the ruins be preserved as a symbol of peace. That is illogical." Tourists with cameras are noisily taking photographs of the Catholic faithful conducting Mass, and a young couple are giggling like visitors to a zoo. The other Catholic again blames this on Tsuyama.

'If this is really a holy place steeped in blood and tearful prayer, why did the atomic bomb explode here? At 11:02 in the morning on August 9, 1945, 8,500 of the 12,000 parishioners in the Urakami diocese perished. Why did the atomic bomb explode over this holy place chosen by Christ the Savior?' Tsuyama is confused; he can't remember if these words came to mind at the time or only now, four years later. It surprises him to be suddenly unable to distinguish between memory and imagination. Perhaps his dead mother had been an Urakami Christian …

This novel captures on various levels the hardships and emotional conflict imbuing life in Urakami after the atomic bombing. It relies on the medium of literature to express facts that would otherwise be difficult to convey. Any attempt to faithfully observe the past demands awareness that one might be overlooking entangled priorities, concealed miseries, and divisions and contempt lurking among people. We must realize with caution that there are human emotions that run too deep to fathom and realities so complicated that we can never expect to unravel them.

Recorded facts are assembled upon the unrecorded vastness of life experience. The reality of the past—the memories of living as though crawling on the ground—fade from our lives in proportion to the passage of time. The absence of the ruins of Urakami Cathedral itself is a fact threatening to fade from human memory. When, confronting this predicament we try to imagine and review the various thoughts and situations of Urakami, works of art like the novel *Chi no Mure* provide us with doorways to the truth. If we want to revisit the past and all the complicated threads of life woven through it, a past that cannot be envisioned merely by inquiry into historical records, it may be necessary to reassemble the facts using the images conjured up in these works of art as tracers.

The reconstruction of Urakami Cathedral began concurrently with the demolition and removal of the ruins of the old building in March 1958 and reached completion in October the following year.

By 1982, Nagasaki was the largest Catholic diocese in Japan with 1,590 households and 8,944 parishioners. The previous year, Pope John Paul II had visited the city in response to a request from the Nagasaki diocese, and Urakami Cathedral had been refurbished to commemorate the event, its roofs plated with copper and exterior walls covered with red brick façades. This is the Urakami Cathedral that we see today.

The photograph used on the cover of the present book shows children playing happily near the ruins. Most of them were probably born in Urakami after the atomic bombing and grew up there later. The children are literally shining with life, and, in the background, the broken walls of the old cathedral and scarred statues of the saints seem to be embracing them with loving smiles. Hidden in the shadows of the ruins—and joining in the joy and laughter of the children—are the spirits of the people who lived in Urakami during the Edo Period, thrived in later decades, and perished along with their church 65 years ago.

For 13 years, the carcass of Urakami Cathedral stood on the hillside watching over the lives of the people, its wounds from the atomic bombing shockingly evident. Chipped and scorched, the statues of the saints also silently conveyed the reality of the atomic bombing. The people of Urakami, meanwhile, looked up at the ruins and recalled the ancestors who made this place their home and who brought the majestic cathedral to fruition. The encouragement they received was profound and immeasurable.

The atomic-bombed ruins of Urakami Cathedral did not persist in concrete form. However, when we look at the visions recorded in this book and hold them up to the light of history, we feel certain that the cathedral is living on in a different form.

Further Reading in English

Boxer, C. R. *The Christian Century in Japan 1549–1650*. Berkley: University of California Press, 1951.

Marx, Joseph Laurance *Nagasaki: The Necessary Bomb?* New York: The Macmillan Company, 1971.

Committee for the Compilation of Materials on Damage Caused by the Atomic Bombs in Hiroshima and Nagasaki (ed.) *Hiroshima and Nagasaki: The Physical, Medical, and Social Effects of the Atomic Bombings*. Tokyo: Iwanami Shoten, 1981.

Nagasaki International Culture Hall (ed.), Brian Burke-Gaffney (trans.) *Nagasaki Speaks: A Record of the Atomic Bombing*. Nagasaki, 1993.

Jenkins, Rupert (ed.) *Nagasaki Journey: The Photographs of Yosuke Yamahata, August 10, 1945*.* San Francisco: Pomegranate Artbooks, 1995.

Dower, John W. *Embracing Defeat: Japan in the Wake of World War II*. New York: The New Press, 1999.

Nagasaki National Peace Memorial Hall for the Atomic Bomb Victoms (ed.), Brian Burke-Gaffney (trans.) *The Light of Morning: Memoirs of the Nagasaki Atomic Bomb Survivors*. Nagasaki, 2005.

---

* Army publicist Yamahata Yosuke entered Nagasaki on the day after the atomic bombing and took dozens of photographs of the devastated city. These provide an invaluable record when, due to the strict censorship imposed by the Occupation government, very few photographs of Nagasaki remain from the postwar period.

あとがき
Postscript

[高原 至]

　昭和12年に長崎県立長崎中学校に入学して以来5年間、放課後、友人の陸上選手の練習を応援するために、浦上天主堂脇の医科大学（現長崎大学医学部）運動場へ良く行ったものだ。カメラをポケットに忍ばせて周辺を散策したが、その時は天主堂へ入ったことはなかった。出会う人々から、他所者がやって来た、という感じで見られることが不思議で、たとえば大浦天主堂一帯とは別世界であった。大浦天主堂へは、クリスマスの時期になると写真仲間と訪れて、その雰囲気を味わい、とても親しみを感じていた。

　昭和20年8月の被爆後、報道の仕事で、浦上を中心とした4,5キロ四方の悲惨な被害状況を撮影して廻ったが、その時にも特に浦上天主堂を重点的に撮影したわけではなかった。

　昭和24年5月、聖フランシスコ・ザビエルの聖右腕が大浦天主堂に数日安置された時、物珍しさ半分で撮影した。聖右腕は、ザビエル祭式典の当日朝、浦上天主堂の倒壊から免れた壁面に安置された。それから大浦天主堂へ移動し、さらに夕方には二十六聖人殉教地の仮安置所でのミサに移された。ものすごい数の信者たちがミサを捧げられる情景に触れて以来、いつの間にか倒壊した浦上天主堂に魅かれ始め、何かに導かれるようにしばしば訪れるようになり、倒壊から免れた天主堂が撤去されるまで撮影していた。

　その後、撮影の仕事で、聖フランシスコ・ザビエルの鹿児島上陸から京都までの道行を辿り、そしてザビエルの誕生したスペインのハビエル城を数回訪れることにもなった。振り返ってみると、ザビエルの導きで浦上天主堂の遺構を撮影していた気がしてならぬ。不思議なご縁であったと思わざるを得ない。

[Takahara Itaru]

　For five years after entering Nagasaki Middle School in 1937 I often went to the Nagasaki Medical College (present-day Nagasaki University Faculty of Medicine) sports field, located beside Urakami Cathedral, to cheer for my friends participating in track and field events. I walked around the area with a camera in my pocket but never actually went inside the church. It was odd to feel as though people were regarding me as a stranger. In this sense Urakami Cathedral seemed to exist in a different realm from Oura Catholic Church. At Christmas time, I went to Oura Catholic Church with my photography pals and basked in the exotic atmosphere, feeling a close familiarity.

　After the atomic bombing in August 1945 I visited the Urakami area as a photojournalist and took photographs of the terrible destruction over a large area. However, I did not particularly concentrate on the ruins of Urakami Cathedral at that time.

　In May 1949, when the holy relic of St. Francis Xavier's right forearm was enshrined at Oura Catholic Church, I took a number of photographs mostly out of curiosity. On the morning of the celebration, the relic was enshrined at the ruins of Urakami Cathedral. After that, the reliquary was moved to Oura Catholic Church, and then to the site of the martyrdom of the Twenty-Six Saints of Japan. The scene of the huge congregation gathered for Mass moved me so much that I began to take a keen interest in the ruins of Urakami Cathedral. As though drawn by some invisible force, I visited the site repeatedly and took photographs until the ruins were finally demolished and removed.

　Over the following years I had the opportunity to

retrace in photographs the steps of St. Francis Xavier from his landing place in Kagoshima to Kyoto. On several occasions I also visited the Xavier family castle in Spain, where the saint was born. I cannot help but think that it was through the guidance of St. Francis Xavier that I pointed my camera again and again at the ruins of Urakami Cathedral. It is indeed a remarkable connection.

*

[ブライアン・バークガフニ]

　日本語には翻訳しがたい言葉がある。「縁」という語もそのひとつであり、それは、人々を結びつけ、人間社会の目に見えないネットワークを形作るような、絆や関係、類似といったようなものを指し示す。本書は、私にとって「縁」に満ちたものである。高原至とは20年以上前からの知り合いであった。かつて彼の会社であるDEITz（旧ナガサキフォトサービス）が製作した本やヴィデオを手伝い、また、高原と故・結城了悟神父による『ザビエルの道』という写真紀行の書物を翻訳する機会にもめぐまれたのであった。

　横手一彦もまた近しい友であり、同僚である。私たちは同じ大学で働き、多くの研究対象を共有している。彼が自らの「あとがき」でも言及しているように、私たちは昨秋、長崎の戦後に関する情報を求めて、メリーランド大学やワシントンD.C.にある国立公文書館で何日か一緒に過ごした。

　こういう次第であるから、本書の翻訳をさせていただいたことは、ある孤立した仕事というよりも、これまで従事してきたことの延長線上にあるもののように感じられる。

　存在していたときも消滅してしまってからも、浦上天主堂の廃墟は、長崎における日本人と外国人コミュニティとを結ぶ「縁」を象徴していたものであり、はじめてポルトガル人宣教師がこの地に足を踏み入れた1567年のあの日にさかのぼらせるものであった。1925年に天主堂が落成を迎えたとき、長崎在住の外国人たち——多くは日本人の隣人とともに規則正しく礼拝に参列しているカトリックであった——は、この日を喜びとともに祝った。わずか20年後にアメリカの飛行機が爆弾を落としてこの聖堂を破壊し、大量のカトリック信者たちが殺されることになろうとは、誰も想像だにしなかったに違いない。その知らせを聞いた誰もが「説明不可能」の一語を口にしたであろう。原子爆弾を生き延びた人たちが後に記した手記にもまた、「筆舌に尽くしがたい」とか「言葉を失う」といったような表現がちりばめられていた。

　幸いなことに、「百聞は一見に如かず」である。本書の写真群は、時間や言語、そして文化の間に立ちはだかる壁を越えて、説明不可能なことがらについて説明しようとする筆者と翻訳者の企てを助けてくれる。

　この機会——「縁」というものを再確認するのみならず、長崎の歴史がもつ深さと大きさ、そして長崎が世界に発するメッセージの重要さに今ひとたび驚かされるという機会を与えてくれた、高原至、横手一彦、そして岩波書店のスタッフに謝意を表したい。

[Brian Burke-Gaffney]

　Some Japanese words defy translation. One of these is the noun *en*, which refers to the links, relationships and similarities that connect people and form the invisible network of human society. For me the present book is rich in *en*. I have known Takahara Itaru for more than 20 years, having enjoyed the opportunity to assist in several books and videos produced by his company DEITz (formerly Nagasaki Photo Service) and even to translate a photographic essay by Mr. Takahara and the late Fr. Yuki Ryogo entitled *The Way of Xavier*.

　Yokote Kazuhiko is also a close friend and colleague. We work at the same university and share many research interests. As he mentions in his postscript, we spent several days together last autumn looking for information about postwar Nagasaki at Maryland University and the National Archives in Washington D.C.

In this way, my involvement in the present endeavor feels more like an extension of previous engagements than an isolated undertaking.

In both their existence and disappearance, the ruins of Urakami Cathedral represented an *en* that united the Japanese and foreign communities of Nagasaki and reached back to the day in 1567 when the first Portuguese missionaries stepped ashore here. When the cathedral reached completion in 1925, the foreign residents of Nagasaki—many of whom were Catholics attending religious services regularly with Japanese neighbors—joyfully celebrated the occasion. None could have imagined that only two decades later a bomb dropped from an American aircraft would destroy the cathedral and kill a large proportion of the Catholic population. Any who heard the news later probably used the word "inexplicable" in reaction. Subsequent writings by atomic bomb survivors are also scattered with expressions like "beyond description" and "lost for words."

Fortunately, one picture is worth a thousand words. The photographs in this book transcend the barriers of time, language and culture and facilitate the attempt of the author and translator to explain the inexplicable.

I would like to thank Takahara Itaru, Yokote Kazuhiko, and the staff of Iwanami Shoten for giving me the opportunity, not only to reconfirm *en*, but also to marvel once again at the depth and breadth of Nagasaki history and the importance of its message to the world.

*

[横手一彦]

2009年の始め頃、職業別電話帳を頼りに、その記載順に電話を掛けた。長崎の敗戦期関連の資料を求め、それがどこかに保存されていないか、何か手掛かりを与えてくれる方がいないかというような、当て処のない問い合わせのためであった。電話口で、露骨に、困惑や嫌悪を示されたこともあった。手前勝手な話に対する当然の対応であり、こちらの非礼を詫びた。空振りの日々が続いた。

ある日、このことを聞き及んだ方から、私の研究室を訪ねたいとの連絡が入った。彼が持参したのは、自身が撮影した記録写真であった。それらは、被爆後の旧浦上天主堂と浦上の人びとの姿を、確かな技量とわかる枠組みのなかにしっかりと写し撮っていた。その構図には、温かな眼差しも感じられた。

本書の発端は、その人——高原至と出会い、その未公開写真の提供を受けたことによる。同じ長崎市に生活していながら、カメラマン高原の仕事を知らなかった。今では、それを恥じるばかりである。

高原の父・高原憲は、医師であり、病院経営者であったため、長崎市に聖母の騎士修道院を創立したマキシミリアノ・マリア・コルベ神父と交友があった。1936年にポーランドへ帰国したコルベ神父は、後にナチ批判の罪でアウシュビッツ強制収容所に送られ、助命を哀訴する収容者の身代わりを申し出て餓死刑に処された。また高原憲は、長崎医科大学放射線医局助教授永井隆の下で、一年余り学んだ若き医師秋月辰一郎を、1944年、浦上第一病院の医長に派遣した。秋月は、被爆直後の浦上で、病舎が焼け、医療機器も薬品も燃え尽きたなか、筵を引いた応急の救護所を作り、素早い医療活動をおこなった。被爆医師秋月は、その後の半世紀にわたって被爆者の治療や証言運動などに携わり、多くの人に信頼され、慕われた。高原至の背景には、このような人びとのつながりが広がっていた。また、本書解説に記した山口愛次郎長崎司教や石田壽とも知り合いであった。

それから半年が経ち、2009年7月14日から8月2日まで、長崎市松ヶ枝のピース・ミュージアムで「幻の世

界遺産——被爆遺構・旧長崎浦上天主堂の記録」と題した 48 点の写真展を開催した。写真選定や会場の確保、写真パネル制作など、準備の時間が足りず、開催までの道のりは平坦ではなかった。幸いこの写真展は、長崎という一地域を越えた反響を呼んだ。来場された方々が、高原の確かな仕事に、被爆後、この地に流れた時空間や人びとの生きる力を感じ取り、心を寄せて下さったからなのだろう。この企画展の写真をあらためて選び直し、さらに数十点を加えて構成されたのが本書である。

本書は、いわば高原の世代が経験したことの上に成立している。そこには、65 年という時間の経過があり、そのことが実感的な把握を困難にしている溝のようにも感じられることもある。しかし私たちは、その意志を持てば、祖父母たちの肉声を聞き、その語りを直接に受け止めることが出来る最後の世代なのである。このことは、沖縄の地上戦も、都市の空襲も、あるいはアジア諸国で展開した戦闘も同様である。この、現在なし得ることを為すことは、10 年後には何ものにも代え難い貴重なこととして振り返られるに違いない。それは、被爆の体験を、キノコ雲の写真のような一瞬の出来事としてではなく、生身の人間がその後に背負った時間として辿り直すことである。それは、どこか遠い過去に、見知らぬ他人に起こったこととしてではなく、私たちは、どれほど痛みを分かち合うことが出来るのか、深くいたわる心で接することが出来るのかという問いの形で、自らの在り方を見つめ直す経験となるであろう。

被爆後の経験の総体——それは死者の無念も含む——を想定する時、言葉が記録した事柄は、その膨大な生きられた時間のごく一部に過ぎない。高原の写真は、このような素朴な事実を教えるのである。被爆天主堂の姿は、13 年という短い間であったが、忍苦を分かち合い、互いに助け合う被爆者たちを見守り続けた。その姿は、傷付きながらも、悲嘆と瓦礫のなかに立ち上がった被爆者たちの生き方に重なる。

本書は、そのような被爆天主堂の最期の姿を記録する。被爆天主堂は、解体撤去され、ついに消滅した。しかし本書の読者の心のなかに、ずっと生き続ける存在であるのかもしれない。

英訳を担ったブライアン・バークガフニは、カナダ生まれの実直な研究者である。2009 年の秋の夕暮れ、10 日ばかりの間、米国内の、とある大学町の居酒屋で、本書の下相談を重ねた。かけがえのない議論であったことを懐かしく思い出し、それが結実したことを喜びたい。

また、編集を担当した大矢一哉に、心からのお礼を申し上げたい。

最後に、写真展開催から本書刊行までの間、多くの方々と諸団体の力添えを得た。名前を記し、謝意を申し上げる次第である。

岩橋謙太郎　大久保一哉　太田純平　大竹豊彦　関口達夫　返田雅之　谷秀樹　中島秀幸　中元英樹　野口勝利　深堀繁美　深堀好敏　前川靖司　増川雅一　松尾隆　松尾緑　水嶋貞夫　森雅治　山下静香　柳時貞　浦上天主堂　長崎原爆資料館　NPO ナガサキピースミュージアム　（財）長崎平和推進協会　DEITz

[Yokote Kazuhiko]

In early 2009 I launched a survey using only a business telephone book as a reference. I randomly dialed one number after another, seeking information about Nagasaki in the immediate postwar period, hoping to find some unknown document or make contact with someone with relevant knowledge. In several cases the person at the other end of the line reacted with blatant but understandable annoyance. I could only apologize for the intrusion. One fruitless week followed another.

One day, however, I received a message from someone who had heard about my inquiry and wanted to visit my office. This person arrived later with a number of photographs that he had taken many years earlier. The photographs captured, with striking skill, the ruins of Urakami Cathedral and the people of the neighborhood after the atomic bombing. They also revealed the humanity and vision of the photographer, Takahara Itaru.

The first seed of the present book was this meeting with Mr. Takahara and his offer to share these unpublished photographs. Although a resident of Nagasaki for many years, I was utterly unaware of Takahara Itaru's photographic achievements. This is now a source of embarrassment.

The photographer's father, the late Takahara Ken, was a physician and administrator of a local hospital who, I learned, had been acquainted with Polish missionary Maksymilian Kolbe, the founder of the Seibono-Kishi (Knights of the Holy Mother) seminary and school in Nagasaki. After his return to Poland, Kolbe was arrested and incarcerated at Auschwitz for criticizing the Nazi regime, and he later volunteered to take the place of a condemned prisoner and died by execution. In 1944, Takahara Ken dispatched a young physician named Akizuki Tatsuichiro to the Urakami Daiichi Hospital, after the latter had studied for a year under the famous Dr. Nagai Takashi, assistant professor of radiology at Nagasaki Medical College. In the aftermath of the atomic bombing, with his hospital and all its medical equipment and supplies reduced to ashes, Akizuki struggled to construct a makeshift relief station from straw mats and to provide early medical attention to the wounded. He remained in Nagasaki until his death more than half a century later, devoting his life to the welfare of the survivors and efforts to convey the reality of the atomic bombing. He was loved and idolized by a whole generation of Nagasaki citizens. These people line up in the background of Takahara Itaru. His acquaintances also include the late Bishop Yamaguchi Aijiro and Ishida Hisashi, mentioned earlier in this work.

From July 14 to August 2, 2009, I arranged with Mr. Takahara to display 48 of the photographs in an exhibition entitled "The World Heritage Site that Never Was: A Record of the former Urakami Cathedral" at the Nagasaki Peace Museum. The preparations for the exhibition were hectic, the time for designation of setting, selection of photographs and creation of explanatory materials anything but sufficient. Fortunately however the success of the exhibition echoed beyond the regional borders of Nagasaki. This was because the people who visited the exhibition were deeply impressed by the scenes of lives and forgotten times captured in Mr. Takahara's photographs. The present book is a new selection of the photographs in the exhibition enhanced with dozens of other photographs unseen to date.

This work is founded on the experiences of Takahara Itaru and other members of his generation. Some 65 years have elapsed, a yawning gap in time that may seem to detract from the reality of those experiences. However, readers will mostly be members of the next demographical group, the last generation blessed with an opportunity to listen to the living words of the atomic bomb survivors. This is an opportunity that we share with the people of Okinawa, with the victims of World War II air raids, and with the people of Asia who suffered from the brutality of war. Indeed, only ten years from now it may be regarded as exceptionally valuable, and its value will lie, not in the recording of momentary events like the mushroom cloud churning up into the sky, but in our reassessment of the terrible burden shouldered by living people in the aftermath. We will enjoy a chance to rethink our own existence, not by looking at events that happened to strangers in some distant past, but by sounding the depths of our capability for compassion and empathy.

Words can capture only a fraction of the experience of the atomic bombing, especially the helpless exasperation of the people who died in that calamity. Takahara Itaru's photographs bring these stark experiences to our attention. Although existent for only 13 years, the ruins of Urakami Cathedral shared in the ordeal of the atomic bomb survivors and watched over their efforts to persevere. The ruins reflected the lives of the survivors, who stood up from the rubble in the atomic wasteland.

The present book records the last days of the cathedral before it was demolished and erased from the face of the earth. In the minds of readers, however, it will probably live on without end.

Brian Burke-Gaffney, who undertook the English translation, is a dedicated scholar and researcher. I had the opportunity to discuss the present undertaking with him during a period of about ten days shared in a certain university town in the United States in the autumn of 2009. I look back with happiness on those discussions and on the impact they exerted on this project.

I would also like to thank to Oya Kazuya, without whose editorial assistance this book would not have seen the light of day.

In conclusion, I would like to express gratitude to the people and organizations that cooperated in the process from photograph exhibition to the present book. The following is an incomplete list: Iwasaki Kentaro, Okubo Kazuya, Ota Junpei, Otake Toyohiko, Sekiguchi Tatsuo, Sorita Masayuki, Tani Hideki, Nakashima Hideyuki, Nakamoto Hideki, Noguchi Katsutoshi, Fukahori Shigemi, Fukahori Yoshitoshi, Maekawa Yasushi, Masukawa Masakazu, Matsuo Takashi, Matsuo Midori, Mizushima Sadao, Mori Masaharu, Yamashita Shizuka, Yu Sijeong, Urakami Cathedral, Nagasaki Atomic Bomb Museum, NP0 Nagasaki Peace Museum, Nagasaki Foundation for the Promotion of Peace, and DEITz.

高原至が中学生時代に撮影した、在りし日の旧浦上天主堂。1936年。

Takahara Itaru took this photograph of the old Urakami Cathedral as a middle school pupil in 1936.

高原 至

1923年長崎県長崎市生まれ。カメラマン。東京写真工業専門学校理学部(現東京工芸大)在学中に学徒兵徴集。大東亜写真協会、毎日新聞西部本社写真記者を経て、ナガサキフォトサービス(現DEITz株式会社)設立。主な仕事に、『ザビエルの道』(DEITz、1988年)、『図説ポルトガル』(高野悦子・伊藤玄二郎編。河出書房新社、1993年)。映像作品では『長崎の印象』(1960年)、『ポルトガル』(1978年)ほか。2020年逝去。

横手一彦

1959年青森県上北郡六戸町生まれ。長崎総合科学大学教授、同大長崎平和文化研究所所長を経て、青森公立大学教授。2025年4月より同大学特別教授。早稲田大学を卒業後、法政大学大学院博士課程単位取得退学。専攻は日本近代文学。主な仕事に『被占領下の文学に関する基礎的研究』論考編／資料編(武蔵野書房、1995-96年)、『敗戦期文学試論』(EDI、2004年)、『被占領下の国語教育と文学』(メリーランド大学図書館ゴードン・W・プランゲ文庫、2009年)、『戦後文学成立期に関する研究』(北方新社、2018年)。

ブライアン・バークガフニ(Brian Burke-Gaffney)

1950年カナダ・ウィニペグ市生まれ。長崎総合科学大学名誉教授、グラバー園名誉園長。専攻は歴史社会学。主な仕事に『花と霜──グラバー家の人々』(長崎文献社、1989年)、『霧笛の長崎居留地──ウォーカー兄弟と海運日本の黎明』(長崎新聞社、2006年)、『欧米人が歩いた長崎から雲仙への道』(フライング・クレイン・プレス、2023年)、翻訳に『長崎被爆記録写真集』(荒木正人監修。長崎国際文化会館、1996年)。

長崎 旧浦上天主堂 1945-58──失われた被爆遺産

	2010年4月8日 第1刷発行
	2025年5月26日 第8刷発行
著訳者	高原 至　横手一彦
	ブライアン・バークガフニ
発行者	坂本政謙
発行所	株式会社 岩波書店
	〒101-8002 東京都千代田区一ツ橋 2-5-5
	電話案内 03-5210-4000
	https://www.iwanami.co.jp/

印刷・三秀舎　カバー印刷・半七印刷　製本・松岳社

© 田中憲一, Kazuhiko Yokote and
　Brian Burke-Gaffney 2010
ISBN 978-4-00-024165-6　　Printed in Japan

原爆体験と戦後日本 ――記憶の形成と継承――	直野章子	四六判 288頁 定価 3520円
図録 原爆の絵 ヒロシマを伝える	広島平和記念資料館編	B5判 182頁 定価 1980円
新版 ナガサキ 1945年8月9日	長崎総合科学大学 平和文化研究所編	岩波ジュニア新書 定価 902円
原爆詩集	峠三吉	岩波文庫 定価 572円
被爆者からあなたに ――いま伝えたいこと――	日本原水爆被害者 団体協議会編	岩波ブックレット 定価 748円
天は語らず	モルガン・スポルテス 吉田恒雄訳	四六判 312頁 定価 3080円

――― 岩波書店刊 ―――

定価は消費税10%込です
2025年5月現在